All the BEST!
Charlie

Indirection

Charles Schlueter

INDIRECTION

On Becoming a Better Musician
and Trumpet Player
As a Conceptual Process

Combray House

Copyright © 2021 Charles Schlueter

All rights reserved. No part of this publication may be reproduced, stored in a retrieval system, or transmitted, in any form or by any means, electronic, mechanical, photocopying, recording, or otherwise, without the prior written permission of the author or publisher. Further information: Combray House, P.O. Box 783, Amherst MA 01004, www.combrayhousebooks.com.

Étude No. 2 *Du Style* from *Trente-Six Études Transcendantes pour Trompette* by Théo Charlier, Copyright (c) 1926 (Renewed) by Éditions Musicales Alphonse Leduc, Paris. This arrangement Copyright (c) 2020 by Éditions Musicales Alphonse Leduc, Paris International Copyright Secured, All Rights Reserved. Reprinted by permission of Hal Leonard LLC.

Musical examples from *Arban's Complete Conservatory Method for Trumpet* are used with the kind permission of Carl Fischer LLC.

Cover sketch by Martha Schlueter; cover design by Ejyo Katagiri; back cover photograph and photos on p. 74 and pp. 151–158 by Eric Berlin; photo on p. 70 by Miriam's mother, Elizabeth Rappaport; photos on pp. 69 and 71 by Hal Oringer; photo on p. 72 by Jack Mohr.

ISBN 978-1-7362292-1-7

Dedication

To Eloise Ristad,
author of *A Soprano on Her Head*

I met Eloise in 1983 and only knew her for two years before her tragic death in 1985. She had a tremendous impact on me—equal to or surpassing that of all of my previous teachers. Eloise was unique in many ways: her perception of what a person needed to improve; her ability to absorb data, process it and know how to use it in a beneficial way. She never used labels: would never say, "Okay, let's try some Feldenkrais, or Alexander technique, or self-hypnosis." She would simply say: "Let's try this or this or ..." Eloise made me aware of how the use of peripheral vision could enhance one's sound. She was the master of using indirection. One of the first things she said to me was: "If you think you have found the answer, you have lost it." Curiosity was her mantra. Just before her death she was studying Jin Shin Jyutsu®, precursor of acupressure and acupuncture. We immediately bonded. We both thought in terms of process, not product. There was never a formula. If I had never met Eloise, I doubt that this book would have ever been written.

Thank you, Eloise.

Contents

Part I: Autobiography 1
    Beginning until Juilliard 3
    Juilliard through Today 10
    Instruments 19
    Influences 20

        first intermission 23

Part II: The Theory in Concept,
Context, and Practice 33
    The Theory in Concept 36
        Shape 36
        Articulation 39
        Grouping 39
    The Theory in Context 40
        Indirection 40
        Learning How, Not Just What, to Think 43
        Relationships 44
        The Learning Modes:
            Aural, Visual, and Kinesthetic 46
        Creating Creative Artists 47
        Developing Technique, Virtuosity, and Music 47
    The Theory in Practice 48
        Charlier #2 48
        Arban Characteristic Study No. 1 58

        second intermission 65

Part III: Principles of the Process 75
    Breathing 77
        Posture 77
        Standing 77

Sitting	78
Misunderstanding	79
Misconceptions	80
Misinformation	81
Avoiding the Panic Zone	82
Tone and Resonance	86
Intonation	88
Embouchure	93
Tonguing	97
Transposition by Clef	102
Rules	109
Shape	110
Articulation	110
Grouping	112
Phrasing	113
Warming Up	122
Practicing	124
Anxiety	132
Auditions	136
Accuracy	140
Dynamics	140
What is the Committee And/or Conductor Looking For?	141
Showing What You Can Do	141
Audition for the Experience?	142
Anxiety and Auditions	142
What to Do?	143
Afterword: The End of the Note	146
third intermission	149
Appendix	159
Essays from Students, Colleagues, and Friends	161
Discography	208
Schlueter Students	218
Just Intonation and Equal Temperament	222
Gustat Warm-ups	224
Recipes	226
Acknowledgements	241

Introduction

The trumpet has been in existence in one form or another for millennia—the earliest trumpets were constructed from animal horns, which eventually gave way to wooden instruments and, ultimately, to the brass instruments we see today. Despite its long and rich history as an instrument of ceremony and communication, the trumpet was not used as a musical instrument until the seventeenth century.

Baroque music is among the most interesting and substantive music we have for the trumpet—from the soaring part in Bach's *Second Brandenburg Concerto* to the brilliant orchestral writing in Handel's *Music for the Royal Fireworks*, the natural trumpet reached its zenith during the Baroque era.

The classical era that followed produced few substantial works for the trumpet. The keyed trumpet, created toward the end of the eighteenth century, yielded concerti by Haydn and Hummel, but little else. Although those works survive, the instrument ended up being short-lived and is rarely utilized today.

The cornet-à-pistons was developed in the 1830s, but trumpets without valves remained until the latter part of the nineteenth century. Thus, the cornet became the solo vehicle for many great virtuosi well into the twentieth century.

Today's trumpets are capable of a wide range of timbre and dynamics, from matching the softest human voice or woodwind to soaring over a big band or symphony orchestra. The trumpet's applications evolved from military to orchestral and then to jazz, chamber music, and an ever-increasing solo repertoire. Trumpets are also made in more keys than any other instrument: B-flat, B-natural, C, D, E-flat, E natural, F, and G; bass trumpet in E-flat, F, B-flat, C, and F-alto; and, of course, the piccolo trumpet in A, B-flat, and C.

Perhaps because the trumpet's solo canon is so much smaller than that of other instruments, pedagogy has long focused on mechanics (embouchure, range, tonguing, flexibility, and endurance) at the expense of musicianship (tone, style, phrasing, nuance, and expression). This book aims to help remedy this imbalance and to provide a framework for young trumpeters to develop their musicianship as they develop their technique and mechanics.

The theory presented in this book has three basic concepts: shape, articulation (or connection), and grouping. Combined, they provide a framework that I hope will not only make it easier to play the trumpet but also easier to play the trumpet musically. It's important to think conceptually. In that sense, much of the most difficult work can be accomplished without ever picking up an instrument—by learning *how* to think instead of *what* to think.

I will also discuss other aspects of playing the trumpet, including breathing, embouchure, tonguing, intonation, phrasing, style, warming up, practicing, transposition, anxiety, and auditions. Some of these concepts may seem self-evident, arbitrary, controversial, or redundant. Regardless of how you respond to what I've written, I hope that you find it thought-provoking and, assuming I have been successful, that you will be inspired to use this book to become a better musician.

This book has been a work in progress for over 40 years, and it is a compilation of what I have learned, observed, and assimilated from relationships with my teachers, students, and many colleagues over the last six-plus decades.

Saint Louis, Missouri, 2020

Part I
Autobiography

Beginning until Juilliard

When I was ten years old, I wanted to play the accordion, probably because my next-door neighbor's grandchildren all played. When my parents took me to the local music teacher, Charlie Archibald, he talked me out of the accordion and suggested I try his cornet, which I did, and I liked it so much that I started taking two lessons a week from him for $0.75 each!

Charlie was a unique person. He had been director of bands in elementary and high schools in Du Quoin, Illinois, but had also worked in the coal mines for many years (that's probably how my father knew him). He was self-taught on all band instruments, and he played a little piano as well. Perhaps because he was self-taught, he didn't ever talk about embouchure or breathing. Instead, he emphasized rhythm (counting) and reading—sight-reading was never mentioned because *everything* I played was for the first time!

I'm pretty sure he had absolute pitch (though I didn't know what that was at the time). I recently learned that during the Great Depression he conducted a Works Progress Administration (WPA) band, and because there wasn't enough money to purchase music, Charlie wrote out all the parts for the band from memory! I should have known this before, because he had written out for me not only popular songs but also solo cornet parts from marches that weren't available.

He had contracted polio a few years before I studied with him and had not been expected to live. Then when he did survive, the prognosis was that he would never walk. By the time I began studying with Charlie, though, he was walking on crutches, about five miles a day, mostly on dirt roads, and before long, he was using only a cane. This was all when he was 70+ years old!

Neither of my parents were musicians, so when they bought my first instrument, they somehow came home with a trumpet instead of a cornet. I have no idea who made that instrument, but on the bell it said, "Elkhart Model," indicating that it had been made in Elkhart, Indiana. I think the trumpet was the more popular instrument, but the cornet soloists of the early twentieth century looked down on the trumpet. Herbert Clarke famously likened the trumpet to the devil, and said that it "is only a foreign fad for the time present." There were some manufacturers (e.g., Olds, Conn) who made cornets that were configured like the trumpet to entice would-be trumpet players to actually play cornets. Unfortunately, modern cornet mouthpieces were usually trumpet mouthpiece cups on a cornet shank, instead of the more conical, funnel shape of the original cornet mouthpieces. The modern flugelhorn mouthpiece has the same shape that cornet mouthpieces used to have.

My father was a coal miner. My earliest encouragement and motivation came from him when he said, "If you learn to play the trumpet, maybe you won't have to work in the mines." He bought two additional trumpets for me after the Elkhart model: the next was an Olds Studio model and, after that, a Leblanc, which he bought when I was a junior in high school. I remember he had to take out a loan to purchase it.

I'm not sure if I ever had a conscious thought that I would pursue playing trumpet as a profession. I think Charlie assumed that I would become a band director, so he began teaching me to read bass clef, as if I was playing a trombone or baritone horn (in other words, a nontransposing instrument). It wasn't until years later, when I learned to read all the clefs and use them for transposing, that I discovered that the way I had learned to read bass clef I was actually reading mezzo-soprano clef!

After studying with Charlie for about three years, my father had the first of many heart attacks. He was unable to work after that, so even $0.75 lessons were more than we could afford, and thus followed a period of about four months when I had no private lessons. About that same time, a new trumpet teacher, Don Lemasters, moved to Du Quoin and started teaching at the local music store, the Egyptian Music Company (Southern Illinois is known as "Little Egypt," thus Southern Illinois University's athletic teams have always been known as the Salukis). Don was from St. Louis, and that is where he had studied with Joseph Gustat, who played trumpet in the St. Louis Symphony Orchestra, mostly as principal, for over 25 years (1920–1946), and Ed Brauer (a protégé of Gustat), who was on staff at NBC Radio. I had heard about Gustat from Charlie because they had played together in their youth. Charlie had always spoken very highly of him, but by the time I started playing, Gustat had retired and moved to Florida. Gustat was the trumpet "guru" in the Midwest, like Max Schlossberg was on the East Coast and Louis Maggio on the West Coast. But Gustat was the teacher players went to study with if they had some problem, like Dizzy Gillespie did when he sort of blew everything out, like Buddy Childers did when he got out of the army and had some problems, and like Rafael Méndez did when he injured his lip (though I understand he attributed his recovery to Maggio).

Don charged $2.50 for lessons. For me that was an astronomical fee, more than three times what I had paid Charlie per lesson each week! As fortune (or good luck) would have it, just before Christmas, the Egyptian Music Company posted a coloring contest in the *Du Quoin Evening Call*, the town newspaper. I won the coloring contest, which entitled me to ten free lessons with Don. He completely overhauled my playing; he changed my embouchure and mouthpiece and taught me about breathing (which had been Gustat's specialty). I must have shown some promise because after the ten free lessons, he continued to teach me for the next five years without charging me.

When I started playing, I had a severe overbite. My top front teeth protruded slightly and had a space between them. Charlie Archibald never mentioned mouthpiece placement, so I placed most of the mouthpiece on my top lip, compensating for restrictions caused by the overbite by accommodating a rather large air pocket in my lower lip.

I did my own orthodontia by using so much pressure on those teeth, thereby pushing the front top teeth back, which also closed up the gap. I managed to develop my range to a D above the staff, and endurance was never an issue. On Saturday mornings, several of Charlie's students gathered at his house for about two hours to play marches by John Philip Sousa, Karl King, Russell Alexander, C. L. Barnhouse, and others. We never gave any thought to developing endurance, we just did it.

I knew nothing about mouthpieces, I just played whatever came with the trumpet. My second trumpet, the Olds Studio model, came with a number 3 mouthpiece. When I began studying with Don, not only did he change my embouchure, but he also gave me a Bach 10½ C, which was huge compared to the Olds 3.

The embouchure change required moving the mouthpiece placement down so that most of it was on my lower lip. Because of my overbite, this also entailed pushing my jaw forward (even when not playing), which I suppose resulted in stretching the tendons. So, without being aware of what Arban advocated (1/3 upper, 2/3 lower), I moved in that direction. Gustat also believed that more of the mouthpiece should be on the lower lip, because the muscles were bigger and could take the mouthpiece pressure, however much that might be. I practiced in front of a mirror for years to observe and to make sure the mouthpiece did not slip back to its original position.

The embouchure change was just one part of the overhaul. In addition to observing my mouthpiece placement, I also had to monitor the placement of my tongue. Gustat advocated keeping the tongue very low in the mouth, and also keeping the soft palate raised in an arch. This had to be checked frequently by looking in the mirror. The reason to strive for this tongue and palate position is to help to keep the resonance the same throughout the entire range of the instrument.

Don also arranged for me to study with Ed Brauer (once he felt it would be beneficial for me to work with Ed). Don offered to pay for my lessons with Ed, but Ed refused to accept payment. Although I had applied to (and was accepted at) the New England Conservatory, Ed said that if I could get into Juilliard and study with William Vacchiano, principal trumpet in the New York Philharmonic, and also get his "blessing," I could be almost assured of having a successful career in the orchestral world. I guess Ed certainly was prophetic, though when I left Juilliard, I didn't know whether or not I had Mr. Vacchiano's blessing.

Another teacher, who was like a second father to me and was the catalyst who helped me integrate what I learned from my first three trumpet teachers, was Mel Siener. Mel became the band director at Du Quoin Township High School about the same time I began studying the trumpet.

He taught me about ensemble playing of many kinds: concert band, dance band, brass quintet and sextet, and trumpet duos and trios. He introduced me to orchestral playing by persuading Maurits Kesner, the conductor of the Southern Illinois Symphony (which was comprised of faculty and students of Southern Illinois University, as well as amateur musicians from the area), to allow me to join the orchestra at age 15. Mel took an immediate interest in me; he gave me the Arban *Complete Conservatory Method*, allowed me to play with his band three years before I got to high school, guided me through my adolescent years, encouraged me during the Juilliard years, and supported me in my early professional years. He also suggested that I join the American Federation of Musicians when I was 15 so that I could play with three different concert bands (affiliated with three AFM locals) during the summers.

After I was admitted to Juilliard, many people advised: "Be sure you get your music education degree because it's not possible to make a living playing!" I didn't know how good one had to be to "make it," and in Du Quoin I think I just assumed that since I played better than my colleagues all those years, it would always be that way. I don't know if it was my own confidence or if it was the confidence that my teachers had in me that caused me to forge ahead, but off I went.

I had no idea what my future would hold when I arrived at Juilliard, although I knew I didn't want to pursue a music education degree: I had seen how Mel had to fight and beg for everything connected to the band. The uniforms were at least 20 years old, and the school-owned instruments were in disrepair. Mel had to do his own repairs because there was no money in the budget for the band. He built the band from about a dozen players to a 65-piece ensemble that performed for all the home football and basketball games, performed four concerts each year, and entered all of the band competitions. Mel allowed only two weeks (ten hours of rehearsals, about the same amount of rehearsal time as professional orchestras) of preparation for any concert or contest; the rest of the time was spent sight-reading whatever was in the band library. Sight-reading was a big part of the band contests. Compared to what we "read" on a regular basis, the "new" pieces were very simple.

Although I had started my own combo when I was in high school, which played for prom and homecoming dances as well as county fairs, I also played with various dance bands in nightclubs. I knew I didn't want to just play "club dates." I never considered trying to break into recording studios because I assumed I would need to improvise, and I had never learned how to "play jazz." I didn't find out until later that the prime requisite for recording work was to be able to sight-read.

Symphony orchestras were not that stable as a means of employment—even the New York Philharmonic only had about a 32-week season in 1957, and the St. Louis Symphony had a 20-week season at about $75.00 a week. Even Bud Herseth finished his master's degree from the New England Conservatory by correspondence after he had become principal trumpet in the Chicago Symphony Orchestra, probably because the season was only around 28 weeks. The major radio and TV studios—NBC, CBS, and ABC— had orchestras and staff musicians in all large cities. The most famous, of course, was the symphony NBC created in New York for Arturo Toscanini. It started out being made up of the staff musicians, and then others were hired from other orchestras. Before Harry Glantz left the New York Philharmonic to become first trumpet in the NBC Symphony, Benny Baker, who was on staff, was the first trumpet.

Juilliard through Today

Studying with Vacchiano was very intense. His primary emphasis was on the tools needed for orchestral playing: tone, rhythm, style, phrasing, and, of course, transposition, which is of prime necessity for orchestral playing and was the most difficult challenge for me.

Juilliard offered coupons to purchase tickets to hear the New York Philharmonic for $0.50. Because I had heard very few symphony orchestra concerts before going to New York, I went to hear them almost every week, sometimes to more than one performance of each program. Hearing Vacchiano in performance was just as crucial to my development as the 45-minute weekly lessons were.

Juilliard offered either a diploma or a Bachelor of Science degree, the latter of which was a five-year course of study, because only 12 academic credits could be taken each year. Although I chose the BS course, I completed it in four years by earning the additional 12 academic credits during two summer school sessions at City College of New York.

I had done reasonably well in high school, but I was unprepared for the level of difficulty of academic and music courses offered at Juilliard. The music curriculum consisted of Literature and Materials, which William Schuman, president of Juilliard, had set up. It covered theory, harmony, and history. There was no textbook for the course; the students created their own by studying the masterworks. There was a separate ear-training class that also included sight-singing. The academic courses were in the humanities, social studies, and history.

I got into the Juilliard Orchestra by accident—Jean Morel, conductor of the orchestra, never accepted me through audition. I was asked to play in an off-stage brass band for a performance of *Job* by Luigi Dallapiccola, conducted by Frederik Prausnitz, assistant conductor. Shortly afterward, one of the trumpet players in the orchestra dropped out of school, and I got in by the back door! I ultimately became principal trumpet when the first trumpet graduated and the next in line after him transferred to the Manhattan School of Music.

Aside from selling my 1951 Chevy to pay for my first year at Juilliard (total tuition was $700—I received a scholarship for $250 and the Chevy covered the other $450), I paid my tuition for the next three years out of what I earned from working in a discount store, singing in church choirs, playing in a band at a summer resort, and some freelancing in New York City with Latin bands and in a few orchestral concerts.

After finishing at Juilliard, I started subbing at Radio City Music Hall. Almost simultaneously with getting hired for the American Ballet Theatre (ABT) Orchestra for a transcontinental tour, I was offered a permanent position at Radio City. I turned down the Radio City position because the ABT was a better job, and my wife, a violinist, was also hired for the ABT tour, so we were "DINKs" (dual income, no kids). Those were the good old days: ABT paid $185.00 per week, but there was no per diem. Radio City paid $140 per week ($7.00 per show × 4 shows per day × 5 days = $140 per week).

The ABT job began with two weeks in New York City. The tour was 20 weeks in two segments: 7 weeks and 13 weeks, with four weeks off in between. All the travel was by bus and most trips were one-nighters, except for those in a few larger cities. The orchestra for the tour consisted of five violins (three firsts, two seconds), one viola, one cello, one bass, one flute, one oboe, two clarinets, two horns, two trumpets, one trombone, one tympanist, and one percussionist. In the large cities, the orchestra was often augmented with extra strings.

The repertoire was extensive: *Billy the Kid*; the Second Act of *Swan Lake*; a ballet called *Gala Performance* that used music from Prokofiev's *Piano Concerto No. 3* and *Classical Symphony*; Chopin's *Les Sylphides*; Meyerbeer's *Les Patineurs*; a work entitled *Etudes* that used the piano music of Czerny (orchestrated by Knudåge Riisager, who composed the *Concertino for Trumpet and Strings*); *Don Quixote* by Ludwig Minkus; and several other works.

Travel was demanding—it wasn't unusual to travel eight hours or more on a performance day, with more travel the following day. Hotels were not expensive, around $5–7 for a double room, but not especially nice either. There were some towns where you could go to any restaurant and get one of everything on the menu for under $20. Although the weekly salary was $185, only 20% was taxed, so the net pay was about $150. Overall, the tour was pretty rewarding—for my wife and me, it was like a six-month honeymoon.

After the ABT tour, I played at the Cape Cod Melody Tent in Hyannis, Massachusetts. Serendipitously, one of Leonard Bernstein's apprentices at the New York Philharmonic had gotten the job as conductor there and needed a principal trumpet. The Melody Tent presented Broadway shows, among them *The New Moon, Gypsy, The Music Man, Bye Bye Birdie, Fiorello!*, and *Brigadoon*.

Following my stint at the Melody Tent, I did a short tour with ABT around New York State. While on that tour, I got called to play as an extra with the New York Philharmonic, conducted by Bernstein, for the opening concert at Lincoln Center's Philharmonic Hall (later renamed Avery Fisher Hall).

After the ABT tour, I played two seasons with the Kansas City Philharmonic. I received my draft notice during the first Kansas City season, so I got a deferment to the end of the season. At that point, I joined the Kansas National Guard, a six-year commitment that included six months of active duty then weekly meetings for the remainder of the six years. I did the six months active duty at Fort Leonard Wood, Missouri, between seasons in Kansas City (the seasons were 24 weeks long).

That first orchestral job was disappointing in many ways. Orchestra contracts at that time generally were vague at best, and demeaning at worst. Except for the so-called "Big Five" orchestras (Boston, New York, Philadelphia, Cleveland, and Chicago), collective bargaining agreements were not negotiated with any input from musicians. Usually, whatever the management decided was approved by the union official and, in most cases, only the management had legal counsel. The Kansas City Philharmonic only had about 12 subscription concerts. Rehearsals were three hours long with an optional five-minute "grace period" before overtime payment could accrue. There were a lot of educational (kiddie) concerts and a lot of run-outs (single out-of-town concerts), as well as short tours. There were also chamber ensembles, including the brass quartet I performed with, that played in schools under the aegis of "Young Audience Concerts," paid for by the Music Performance Trust Fund (which was funded through recording royalties) that the union had negotiated.

Like our contracts, tour conditions were whatever the management decided on. Supposedly, no more than seven hours of travel was allowed on the orchestra's day off, but there were no penalties if the rules weren't followed and there was no travel committee to review the conditions. During my second season, the orchestra had a tour to California and the Pacific Northwest in February; the bus drivers were from Los Angeles. An accident occurred in which one of the buses turned over, resulting in over two dozen serious or life-threatening injuries. Key replacements were hired and the tour resumed, leaving the injured and hospitalized behind. When the subject of penalties for overtime travel was raised, management threatened to stop salaries of injured orchestra members in retaliation.

Even before the accident, I was discouraged by how the management treated the orchestra. Many of the members who had been there for many years and had started families needed to find other means of earning a living during the six months between seasons. There was no unemployment insurance, so we were on our own—some of us drove taxis, others worked in flower nurseries, and one musician was a cartographer! Salaries increased from $97.50 per week to $100 per week the second season I was there, but there were no long-range plans for lengthening the season or increasing compensation.

Overall, morale was not very high. Many fine players spent time with the Kansas City Philharmonic before moving on to better-paying or more stable jobs, including Philip Farkas (horn) and Donald Peck (flute), who eventually became mainstays in the Chicago Symphony Orchestra. I stopped practicing after I got out of my six months of active duty. I would come home from rehearsal, make a martini, and watch cartoons on a black-and-white TV. I was ready to go back to New York and either freelance or change to a different career.

Around this time, I found out about an opening in the Milwaukee Symphony Orchestra and decided to take the audition. In those days there were no repertoire lists—you would take in a pile of excerpt books and tell the committee what you intended to play. I began practicing again, but I couldn't even get through what I chose to play. To this day I have no idea what the committee heard in me, but I was offered the job!

In those days, the union locals in many cities put a restriction on players imported from outside the immediate area. Imported players were not allowed to play any other jobs outside of the orchestra during what was usually a two-year "transfer" period. However, once I resigned from the Kansas City Philharmonic, I was allowed to play the Starlight Theatre in Kansas City (similar to The Muny in St. Louis), which presented Broadway shows during the summer.

I played in the Milwaukee Symphony Orchestra for three years. It had a 28-week regular season, but no summer season. Fortunately, there was a local tent theater presenting Broadway shows, just like the Cape Cod Melody Tent, and I played there for three summers.

Shortly after I was hired in Milwaukee, I was first offered assistant principal trumpet and then principal trumpet in the Israel Philharmonic, both of which I turned down. I also took auditions for other orchestras, including the Detroit Symphony. Frank Kaderabek won the Detroit position, leaving a position open in the Chicago Symphony Orchestra, for which the entire Milwaukee trumpet section auditioned.

I also auditioned for principal in the St. Louis Symphony Orchestra. It wasn't advertised, but I found out about it from Ed Brauer, and I more or less set up the audition myself. Since they weren't really prepared to have an audition, I was "hired" to play a short tour as a paid audition. The morale in that orchestra wasn't much better than the morale in Kansas City. Suffice it to say, I didn't end up taking that job.

During my third year in Milwaukee, I was invited to audition for the Cleveland Orchestra and won that audition. I promised myself that if I were to leave New York, it would only be to take principal trumpet positions. However, the Cleveland Orchestra, conducted by George Szell, had a great reputation, and with its year-round season, I figured it would be worth going back on that promise. My contract read, "Assistant/Associate/Alternate First, Third, Fourth and Cornet"! It wasn't long before I realized that I preferred playing principal.

After five years in Cleveland, I auditioned for, and won, the principal trumpet position with the Minnesota Orchestra (formerly the Minneapolis Symphony Orchestra), which allowed me to return to my self-imposed promise. That was the first audition I'd ever taken in which the final round was playing in the orchestra during a rehearsal. If it hadn't been done that way, I probably wouldn't have won! I was principal trumpet for nine years and was on the faculty of the University of Minnesota during that time.

In 1979, when Armando Ghitalla retired as principal trumpet of the Boston Symphony Orchestra, I was called by the personnel manager, who invited me to audition. I told him I was happy in Minneapolis and was not looking for another job. I also let him know I wasn't interested in playing a "naked audition" (just playing excerpts for a committee), but I would consider flying to Boston to play with the orchestra if the BSO paid my expenses. Unfortunately, their contract would not allow that.

Two years later, when Rolf Smedvig decided to leave the BSO, the personnel manager again called to invite me to audition. This time, however, the BSO would pay my expenses and I would play with the orchestra in a rehearsal situation. The committee did insist that I also play the "naked audition." I agreed, but only if I would first play with the orchestra.

Thus, in 1981, I joined the Boston Symphony Orchestra as principal trumpet. I held that position for 25 years until retiring in 2006. I was the only principal trumpet of the BSO in the 20th century who was brought in from outside the orchestra—every other principal had joined the orchestra as third and assistant principal trumpet (with the notable exception of Georges Mager, who came in as a violist).

Back in high school, predictions were made as to what everyone would be doing in 25 years: I'd be working for the Argonne National Laboratory in Chicago and playing principal trumpet in the Boston Symphony Orchestra "on the side." So, I sort of fulfilled half of that prophecy.

☐

My position in the Boston Symphony Orchestra led to many other opportunities, including an appointment to the faculty of the New England Conservatory, where I taught for 31 years. Touring the world with the orchestra and as a member of the BSO Chamber Players helped to attract many talented international students to my studio at NEC and led to my being invited to teach abroad. For many years, I was a visiting professor at Kurashiki Sakuyo University in Kurashiki, Japan, and I continue to teach and play in Brazil as I have since 1988. Closer to home, I was a visiting professor at the University of Connecticut for a year. I have recorded six solo albums: *Bravura Trumpet, Virtuoso Trumpet, Trumpet Concertos, Trumpet Works, Songs from the Heart,* and *Statements.*

In 2001, I established The Charles Schlueter Foundation with the mission to foster the enjoyment of music, promote music education, assist in the training of talented young brass performers, encourage improved brass pedagogy, and support the creation of new literature for brass instruments. Specifically, the foundation's aims are:

- To establish international collaboration in the field of musical performance
- To celebrate and preserve the cultural and artistic heritage of the trumpet and its repertoire
- To support and encourage the creation of new solo and ensemble literature for the trumpet
- To inspire and guide emerging talented trumpet performers toward professional achievement
- To record important trumpet repertoire for posterity
- To encourage the study of the trumpet
- To promote music as an essential part of school curricula
- To maintain an effective liaison with various schools, communities, and national organizations that have allied interests in music and music education
- To understand and demonstrate how music serves as a means of communication across a range of cultures throughout the world
- To present recitals at community venues other than major performance centers

Although I eschewed getting a degree in music education, teaching has always been important to me, and my relationships with students have been a part of my learning process. During my student days at Juilliard, I thought if I could combine everything I learned from all my teachers, it would provide a framework for passing on my cumulative knowledge.

Instruments

The last trumpet my father bought for me, the Leblanc B-flat, was stolen in the summer of 1959 in Du Quoin. I replaced it with another Leblanc B-flat. Those were the only trumpets I owned until my last year at Juilliard, when I bought a French Besson C trumpet from Mr. Vacchiano. I also bought a Mahillon D trumpet that year.

After hearing Armando Ghitalla play Martin trumpets in a recital at Carnegie Recital Hall in 1961, I acquired a set of Martin trumpets in C, D, and B-flat. I used those until 1965, when I switched to Getzen trumpets. Getzen made me a C trumpet, and I helped them design a D trumpet modeled after the Martin D.

After joining the Cleveland Orchestra (an audition I won playing the Getzen C trumpet), I was advised that I should get a Bach. Thus began my involvement with instrument modification. Probably because I was in the Cleveland Orchestra, the people at Bach (which was owned by Selmer) accommodated my request to make some changes in their basic C trumpet design. I started with a longer leadpipe—copied from the dimensions of the Getzen. This further evolved to a full B-flat leadpipe and, along the way, caused Bach to make other models that were variations based on my suggestions.

Shortly before leaving Minneapolis, I met David Monette who, at the time, was doing instrument repair in Salem, Oregon. He started designing his own leadpipes and building his own trumpets in 1983. Since then, I have played only Monette trumpets and am now regularly associated with his instruments. William Vacchiano was associated with Vincent Bach; Joe Gustat was associated with C. G. Conn; Gustav Heim with Holton; Rafael Méndez with Olds; etc.

Influences

My theory of trumpet playing as a conceptual process is a culmination of what I learned from my trumpet teachers, from other musicians, and from my experience performing and teaching over several decades.

My first teacher, Charles Archibald, was self-taught. He never talked about embouchure or breathing, just reading and rhythm. Don Lemasters emphasized sound, breathing, embouchure, and articulation. Ed Brauer emphasized concept of tone, intonation, breathing, range, endurance, and attitude about performing. William Vacchiano emphasized tone, rhythm, style, phrasing, transposition (a necessity for orchestral repertoire, but also for using trumpets pitched in different keys), and musicality.

In addition to my teachers, there were many other musicians who influenced me, most of whom I wasn't aware of until much later. For instance, long before I'd had any thoughts of becoming a musician, I listened to *Your Hit Parade* on the radio and heard the great pop singers of the time: Frank Sinatra, Tony Bennett, Rosemary Clooney, Doris Day, Dinah Shore, and others.

Of course, I also heard many trumpet players in live performances: William Vacchiano, Ed Brauer, Armando Ghitalla, Roger Voisin, Adolph Herseth, Maynard Ferguson, Louis Armstrong, and Doc Severinsen, to name just a few. On recordings, I listened to Harry Glantz (NBC Symphony, New York Philharmonic), Georges Mager (Boston Symphony Orchestra), Harry James, Conrad Gozzo, and Fritz Wesenigk (Berlin Philharmonic). They each had a unique sound that made an indelible impression on me. Vacchiano encouraged me to listen to string quartets, both in concert and on recordings, and I also listened to recordings of great operatic singers like Enrico Caruso, Beniamino Gigli, Maria Callas, and Renata Tebaldi.

My cumulative learning from all of the above influenced how I think about sound, phrasing, nuance, inflection, expression, interpretation, and style—the mosaic of music. Proverbially, *the whole is greater than the sum of its parts.*

first intermission

Charlie Archibald, my first teacher, looking like he's ready for a parade. I had trouble counting eighth notes with my foot, so he would actually beat my foot for me. He also didn't believe in valve oil. Instead, he would spit on the valves, and since he chewed tobacco laced with oil of wintergreen, the valves deteriorated rapidly. To this day, whenever I smell oil of wintergreen, I remember Mr. Archibald.

Don Lemasters, Ed Brauer, and me in St. Louis in 1973. I am playing a King miniature piccolo B-flat, which I bought from Ed more than a decade later.

Left to right, I am with Wally Clark, Merrill Emling, Richard Allen, Ross Mayor, and Richard Haines in our 1956 combo.

Here I am in 1959 in my hometown of Du Quoin, with my new moustache and second Leblanc B-flat; the first Leblanc I owned, which my father had bought me, was stolen from my borrowed car while I was having coffee at a Walgreens.

It's 1962 and I am playing my newly acquired Martin Custom Committee C trumpet as principal trumpet in the Kansas City Philharmonic.

Milwaukee, Wisconsin in 1965 finds me in the U.S. Army Reserves of Wisconsin, which I had joined in 1963 after receiving a draft notice. I was discharged in 1969.

With Rick Metzger in the Milwaukee Symphony: I had switched to Getzen trumpets, and like a good colleague, Rick did too. If memory serves, this photo was taken in 1966, when we performed the Vivaldi Concerto in C Major for two trumpets.

With the Cleveland Orchestra in 1971, sporting the beard I was allowed to grow after Maestro Szell's death (he permitted only sideburns and moustaches).

It's 1972 and I have become principal trumpet of the Minnesota Orchestra, a position I held until leaving for Boston in 1981.

Serenading my "adopted" Trumpeter Swan in Minneapolis in 1981. The Minnesota Zoo had a program for people and groups to adopt an animal. The Women's Committee of the orchestra adopted a Trumpeter Swan and wanted to name it Charlie Tooter, but the zoo said no, so instead I played at the adoption "dedication." Trumpeter Swans are beautiful to look at but rather nasty creatures!

Part II
The Theory in Concept, Context, and Practice

Theory: an educated guess about the nature of the problem.

—Murray Bowen

There have been many theories of trumpet (or cornet) playing over the last 150 years, including notable ones by J. B. Arban, Herbert Clarke, Walter Smith, Louis Maggio, Joseph Gustat, Arnold Jacobs, Roy Stevens, William Costello, Donald Reinhardt, Carmine Caruso, James Stamp, and Vincent Cichowicz. Many of these have focused on embouchure, range, technique, and flexibility, although a few (notably those by Gustat and Jacobs) have focused on breathing and the use of air.

I hope to add to that tradition by providing a framework for thinking about music as a conceptual process, to integrate theory with method and technique in a way that prioritizes musicians' ability to think for themselves. A useful parallel can be found in the two types of reasoning: deductive and inductive. Deductive reasoning is narrower and is generally used to test or confirm hypotheses. Inductive reasoning is more open-ended and exploratory. Trumpet players are too often taught *what* to think, not *how* to think. This focus on deductive reasoning, at the expense of inductive reasoning, is antithetical to creative music-making. Learning *how* to think with imagination through inductive reasoning will ultimately be of greater benefit to the musician. Although my playing career has been predominantly orchestral, through my teaching I've found this approach to be helpful for musicians of any genre: classical (solo, orchestral, chamber), jazz, modern, and even commercial music.

My approach to playing and teaching is through process, not product. This creates a paradox: writing this book becomes the product, a product that aims to describe the process! In attempting to deal with the whole, which is greater than the sum of its parts, I have to deal with the parts and details, at the same time trying to avoid being overly analytical and losing sight of the whole.

And so, we begin.

The Theory in Concept

Shape • Articulation • Grouping

In no particular order, because they all occur simultaneously.

My theory of trumpet playing, encompassing shape, articulation, and grouping, might be filed into a mental folder labeled ***"End of the Note."*** Thinking of the ends of notes is about process—the end of the note includes the beginning and the middle, but without thinking of them. Understanding the difference between *product* and *process* is critical. Thinking of the beginnings of notes will lead one to focus on product, and yet, ironically, there is no product. Whether a note comes out perfectly or imperfectly, it is gone. Even if it is recorded, it exists only as a reproduction.

Shape

The shape of a note consists of several variable qualities, including duration, pitch, intonation, timbre, dynamic, and style. The first two, duration and pitch, are specifically notated by the composer (although the exact duration of the note can change depending on context and interpretation). Assuming just intonation (rather than tempered pitch), intonation will also change with context, which demands the trumpeter have the skill to ensure that slides are moved as necessary.

Timbre can be defined in three different ways: (1) the intensification and enriching of a musical tone by supplementary vibration; (2) a quality imparted to voiced sounds by vibration in anatomical resonating chambers or cavities (such as the mouth or nasal cavity); or (3) a quality of richness or variety. I would add that timbre is intrinsically linked to resonance, specifically the presence and quality of overtones that provide color to the fundamental note. Maximum resonance can be achieved by using one's peripheral vision to project their sound into the distance so the sound expands to fill the space.

Conceptually, there are three types of dynamics: decibel, acoustic, and intensity. Decibel dynamics are the most straightforward and are indicated by the composer, everything from *pp* to *ff* (and well beyond for Tchaikovsky and others!). Acoustic dynamics reflect pitch and range. High notes tend to sound louder, and ascending lines sound as if they're getting louder. Conversely, low notes tend to sound softer, and descending lines sound as if they are getting softer. The entire Arban book is predicated on acoustic dynamics—always crescendo when ascending, either scale or arpeggio, and decrescendo when descending. Intensity dynamics are achieved by increasing the velocity of air to create more brilliance, or by increasing the speed of vibrato while making it narrower. Dynamic intensity can also be achieved rhythmically (shorter notes tend to have more intensity than longer notes) and from articulation (detached notes have more intensity than slurred notes).

Style is relative to the type of music: baroque, classical, romantic, jazz, contemporary. How do we define style in the context of music? Basically, it is a consistency of like patterns: tonal, rhythmic, harmonic, and dynamic. It is necessary to develop an awareness of shape, articulation, and grouping appropriate to each period's style of music. The musician provides the *content*; the composer provides the *context*. The *content* (i.e., the tone, dynamics, and articulation) of the late nineteenth and early twentieth centuries cannot be used in the *context* of baroque or classical music, and vice versa.

Baroque era architecture is easy to describe because it's visual: ornate, ornamented, and extravagant. Because of the limited number of notes available to the baroque trumpet (its range being in the upper tessitura), ornamentation was limited to trills. This trumpet, because of its design, was capable of blending dynamically.

During the classical era, the art of playing the trumpet in the extreme upper register had disappeared: the range of the instrument was confined to the middle of the treble clef, and the trumpet was used primarily as an extension of the tympani. Valves were added to the cornet in the Romantic era (early nineteenth century), and to the trumpet in the middle part of the nineteenth century, meaning composers could now write melodically for these instruments. This, of course, opened up the potential and the necessity for players to become even better musicians.

The advent of jazz in the United States presented new possibilities for making music with the trumpet. The practice of ornamentation and improvisation, discarded after the baroque era, was rediscovered. Many contemporary composers have incorporated, and even merged, jazz idioms into their compositions, so an awareness of all styles and periods of music is an essential part of becoming a better musician.

Articulation

Trumpet players tend to think of articulation as tonguing, and slurring as the absence of tonguing. In reality, articulation is the way in which notes are connected, either by sound (slur, portamento) or by silence. A slur is the sound that connects notes of different pitch. Notes connected by silence are harder to describe. A rest is a notation for silence, but notes that are not connected by sound (not slurred) are either legato or staccato (Italian) or *detaché* (French).

Grouping

Regardless of style, musical ideas almost never occur within beams, bar lines, or articulation markings. Notes that occur on inner or weaker subdivisions should be inflected as a musical phrase to the next beat or subdivision. I call this grouping.

If all notes are on the beat, then the next hierarchy is used. For example, in 2/4 time, the grouping should be 2-1; if the meter is 3/4, the grouping should be 2-3-1; if the meter is 4/4 the grouping should be 2-3 and 4-1; and so on.

There is an excellent book by James Morgan Thurmond entitled *Note Grouping: A Method for Achieving Expression and Style in Musical Performance*. Since this book was originally written as a thesis for a college degree, Thurmond goes into great detail about note grouping and provides extensive historical and musical justifications and examples for using this approach. He uses the terms *arsis* and *thesis* to explain the roles of the upbeat and downbeat in grouping. Arsis is likened to the motion of lifting one's foot before stepping, and thesis is likened to stepping.

The Theory in Context

Many of the greatest trumpet players have played with embouchures or techniques that shouldn't have "worked," but they overcame physical limitations to succeed musically—often in spite of what they did as much as because of what they did. The overriding factor was their concept of music.

The relationship between a musician and their instrument is just that, a relationship. Like all healthy relationships, accommodation and adaption are critical. Musicians who overcome physical limitations to succeed musically do so because they are skilled at accommodating and adapting. My approach to playing the trumpet and making music is rooted in relationships and, in a sense, this book is about providing a framework for approaching the instrument in a more meaningful and adaptive way that is more about music and less about mechanics—in other words, relating all the components.

Indirection

Indirection is an indirect procedure or action. It is a powerful tool for learning, teaching, and connecting all the parts that make up the whole. My theory is to use indirection to encourage induction (learning how to think) rather than deduction (learning what to think). Induction allows the use of unconscious wisdom and ability through following a general framework or process. Using this conceptual process of induction increases the probability of achieving one's goals by facilitating the connection between thinking and doing, whereas deduction uses the conscious mind to find answers, orienting oneself around the product. Examples of indirection have been expressed and reflected in great thinkers from many different cultures throughout history:

- Sufi saying:
  - If you want the door to listen, talk to the window, and vice versa.
- Milton Erickson:
  - Depotentiate the conscious mind.
  - Use unconscious wisdom at every opportunity.
- Albert Einstein:
  - Imagination is more important than knowledge.
  - Education is what remains after one has forgotten everything he learned in school.
  - We cannot solve our problems with the same thinking we used when we created them.
- Michelangelo:
  - Every block of stone has a statue inside it, and it is the task of the sculptor to discover it.

The greater danger for most of us lies not in setting our aim too high and falling short, but in setting our aim too low and achieving our mark. This sentiment, too, has been repeated by great teachers throughout history:

- Moshe Feldenkrais:
  - I am going to be your last teacher. Not because I'll be the greatest teacher you may ever encounter, but because from me you will learn how to learn. When you learn how to learn, you

will realize that there are no teachers, that there are only people learning and people learning how to facilitate learning.
- Eloise Ristad:
  - If you think you have found the answer, you have lost it.
  - If you are worried about missing a note, miss the first one—get it out of your system!
  - If you are worried about missing a note, try to miss it really badly.
  - Command yourself: "Screw up."
- James Stamp:
  - Think down when going up; think up when going down.
- Arturo Toscanini:
  - Tradition is the latest in a string of bad performances.
- Vladimir Horowitz:
  - Perfection is in itself imperfection.
- Carl Schiebler:
  - What works in practice may not work in theory.
- Guy Burton:
  - Never tolerate mediocrity, nor succumb to complacency.
- Balinese Proverb:
  - We have no art; we just do the best we can.

To these, I would add:

- You can learn without understanding and understand without learning.
- You can't learn what you don't already know.
- We know more than we know we know.
- It is better to be a musician first and a trumpet player second.
- Problems are most often symptoms.

- What makes trumpet playing difficult is that it is basically easy.
- Out of chaos comes clarity.
- Poor judgment comes from lack of experience, and experience comes from poor judgment.
- Without establishing content, there can be no differentiation in the context.
- Thinking about the beginning of a note is product; thinking about the end of a note is process.

Learning How, Not Just What, to Think

No one can teach anyone anything; we can only teach ourselves. The best things I can do as a teacher are to challenge a student to think more about *how*—not *what*—to think about music, and encourage them to approach the music with more curiosity and imagination. One of the dilemmas all of us must deal with is that we are taught *what* to think, not *how* to think. This education begins with our parents trying (with good intentions) to teach us what to think and how to act, according to their standards (ethics, morals, beliefs), which of course comes from their parents and grandparents and is passed on through generations. Our education system reinforces deductive thinking by prioritizing answers—*what* to think in a way that centers around memorizing what has already been done.

For children, imagination is a vital part of everyday life. It is how they relate to the world around them, by creating scenarios that include imaginary friends or pretending that their toys can become real. When they begin school, their imagination is inhibited and even discouraged by constant refrains of "Stop daydreaming!" and "Pay attention!" This approach to education has led to a metric for evaluating teachers that is, at best, counterproductive. Public school teachers are judged based on their students' ability to regurgitate facts on standardized exams, while conservatory teachers are judged on how well their students can regurgitate excerpts within the narrow scope of what is now acceptable to advance in and win orchestral auditions.

Relationships

The first breath a newborn child takes sets the stage for life. That breath and all that follow are both involuntary and essential to life (and later, to trumpet playing!). From that first breath, the child begins to build a continuous series of relationships: to their parents, to their siblings, and to the environment. At once the child is special but not special—they are primarily focused on self and how their needs are satisfied but, as the child grows, those needs change along with the means of meeting and satisfying them. In addition to external relationships, the child also develops a relationship between intellect and emotion that will change and evolve throughout the child's life.

When a child begins to play an instrument, they form a new relationship with the instrument and, usually, with a teacher. The teacher serves as the child's first musical relationship. Each new relationship the child makes will modify previous and ongoing relationships. It is the same in the physical world: when different elements combine, they form something new and different.

The trumpet player must adapt to the instrument. A lesser quality instrument will require more adaptation than a superior instrument. The relationship a musician has with their instrument is special—the closer the better—and the instrument amplifying the musician's voice to better connect with the audience is the ultimate goal.

In all relationships (but especially musical relationships), it is necessary for one to accommodate and adapt. The student adapts to or accommodates the teacher, but the teacher must also adapt to and accommodate the student. Ideally these relationships are interdependent and symbiotic, benefiting both parties. They form the basis for relating to the trumpet and to music, like hydrogen and oxygen relating to each other to form water. This is symbiosis. *The whole is greater than the sum of its parts.*

In any relationship, there is always a risk of too much togetherness and sameness. The desire to fit in, to be accepted, liked, and to belong, can be overwhelming in a way that stifles creativity. Anyone who deviates may be criticized, belittled, ignored, or even punished. When one moves out of the fold, anxiety increases in the individual and in the group. Emotions then battle with (and often dominate) rational thought. Ultimately, though, it is the individual who differentiates him or herself from the norm—breaking new ground and making discoveries—who creates new horizons for the group.

The paradox for musicians is that if we attempt to think or do something differently, it makes us uncomfortable, raising the anxiety level both of the player and of the group. A Japanese maxim seems to apply here: *The nail that sticks up, must be hammered down.* An ensemble is a mosaic made of many parts, almost all of them different from the others, that must fit together to complete the picture. Again, the whole is greater than the sum of its parts. As musicians in an ensemble, there are ways that we *must* relate to or fit in with the group—intonation, rhythm, dynamics, blend, timbre, and balance, to name a few, but the individual also has a role in determining these many factors.

The Learning Modes: Aural, Visual, and Kinesthetic

Humans learn cumulatively, gradually developing knowledge and skills over time. There are three basic learning modes: aural, visual, and kinesthetic (physical). Everyone has one that is dominant, but all are used. My dominant learning mode is visual, which explains the visual terminology I frequently use (shape, color, and connection, for example). Trumpet playing is a conceptual process that incorporates all three: aural (music as sound, learned with the ear); visual (learning to read sheet music); and kinesthetic (learning rhythm, but also as a physical phenomenon—what playing a particular note feels like in the muscles).

Ideally, before beginning to play an instrument, one should learn to read music and become fluent in solfeggio so that the ear becomes properly trained. Unfortunately, this happens in only a few countries (e.g., France, Italy, and Spain), and rarely in the United States, where ear training very often isn't studied until the student progresses to a more advanced level in their musical education. I was not introduced to solfeggio and formal ear training until I entered Juilliard.

When a student does begin to learn solfeggio, it is often done with a piano. As a tempered pitch instrument, using a piano to learn solfeggio can cause the student to hear "out of tune," which can hinder the development of any instrumentalist (except a pianist!). When possible, then, a student should learn solfeggio *before* studying piano. Even studying piano without solfeggio will provide a musical foundation. Nevertheless, in many—if not most—cases, students begin to play the trumpet with no prior musical training.

Creating Creative Artists

One usually thinks of creative artists as being painters, writers, or composers. In the world of music, in addition to composers, there are those musicians who are spontaneous composers, who improvise. Today this art belongs almost exclusively to jazz musicians. All other performing musicians must *recreate* what others have composed. However, each and every performing musician is a creative artist; even though they are required to play the music composed by someone else, they do this with their own unique tone, technique, interpretation, style, and expression. To create beautiful music, the musician must use imagination, whether improvising or playing the music of others. The performer must form concepts of the whole, integrating tone, technique, interpretation, style, and expression into the notes being played. It is this conceptual approach to playing the trumpet that I wish to pursue and teach.

Developing Technique, Virtuosity, and Music

For trumpet players, there are many method books, most notably those by Arban, Saint-Jacome, and Clarke, and there are many etude books, including those by Walter Smith (*Top Tones*), Théo Charlier (*Trente-Six Études Transcendantes*), and Edwin Franko Goldman (*Practical Studies*). These books focus primarily on technique, but for me technique is how to play one note and get to the next note (*virtuosity* is, therefore, playing a lot of notes!).

The musician provides the *content* while the composer provides the *context*. The relationship between the two results in *music*. To make music, one needs only the correct utensils (a trumpet, mouthpiece, and sometimes mutes) and well-honed tools (the brain, lungs, embouchure, tongue, and fingers).

The Theory in Practice

Charlier #2*

In my studio, it is not uncommon when a student approaches this etude for the first time for common errors to occur. There is no inflection or direction to the notes; the first F sounds like it starts on the downbeat in bar one. In bar two, the dotted quarter F becomes a downbeat of sorts due to overemphasis. The dotted quarter note ending is not defined, so the following eighth note is not even distinguishable—we failed to prepare the anacrusis, the unstressed note that comes before the next measure. There are two separate phrases: the question and the answer. Now we have made a run-on sentence. All the ingredients are lacking—no inflection or grouping.

---

*Conversation transcribed by Matt Sonneborn

So what is different here? This is where we begin to apply Indirection. Think about grouping *across* the bar line, avoiding the obvious and becoming involved in the process. The first two phrases are now a question followed by an answer, not just a run-on sentence. Pay attention to connecting by sound. Trumpet players have a tendency to slur simply by not tonguing. Instead, make certain the notes that are slurred are connected by sound. Thinking this way incorporates the three basic concepts into the end of the note. By thinking of the end of the note, we actually begin to subconsciously pay more attention to the beginning, the middle, and the end.

The student is still prone to succumbing to obvious traps. In the second bar, the top F will be overly accentuated, causing the bar line to move one beat and making the F beat one of the next bar instead. In the octave slur, the emphasis on the top note is a result of not preparing it with the bottom note. Without defining the anacrusis, everything becomes crunched together. The lack of phrasing would easily be fixed if the student could focus on the end of the note. The eighths tend to be overly long and the differentiation becomes inaudible. Often the sixteenths are compressed or unequal. There may be notes that don't speak (the printed F in bar three, for example) as a result. The rushing of sixteenths is imminent. The student might also be tempted to emphasize the final F in this example, giving the impression of a new bar instead of sounding as it is written on beat 2.

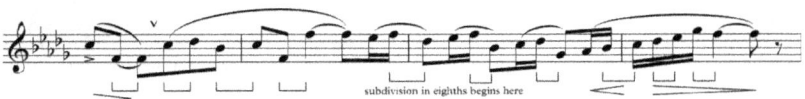

Now let's discuss the indirect approach to interpreting this passage and mending those problematic areas as a conceptual process. By grouping across the pulse and avoiding the obvious traps, the notes become connected by sound, differentiated by shape, and well-defined. Subdividing running sixteenth notes into micro groups prevents the crushing and rushing problem in the prior example. In bar two, we avoid the over-accenting by emphasizing the bottom F, almost as if it were a springboard to the higher octave—it creates energy for the octave slur and the acoustic dynamics lead to equal emphasis. By putting the energy on the bottom note, the top note is no longer overly "obvious," or too loud. At the end of this passage, a crescendo to decrescendo was added, making the F sound as printed, on the second beat instead of as the first beat of a new bar.

The next passage includes more traps, beginning with the first printed F which is often played without a clearly defined end. This can leave the student unprepared for the following C which might not speak and will compromise the phrase. The top F tends to be sharp, leading to a multitude of issues including inconsistent timbre. As before, the student also risks overemphasizing the downbeats. As happened earlier in the etude, overemphasizing the bottom F may again give the false impression that the meter is 4/4 rather than 3/4. Without realizing it, the student will focus on product and the sixteenth passages become pedantic "pogo sticks" at the expense of thoughtful phrasing. Complicating matters, this section centers around the dominant of B-flat minor and, without proper attention to intonation, results in playing higher on the pitch. Lower neighbors should be treated as the 3rd of the dominant (lowered) to achieve proper intonation. Bar three is often played with an overemphasis on the eighth notes (despite the printed staccatos).

Let's talk about this section in depth. The groupings we have discussed prior are again illustrated. You will also notice some arrows which indicate the lowering of pitch with slides. It is necessary to hear these notes as "lower neighbors" in order to play them correctly in tune. The issues that were product-oriented have now been addressed with brackets to indicate note grouping. The decrescendo has been added to avoid the overemphasis of the notes that follow. Thinking of the end of the note includes how the notes are shaped, grouped, and connected.

This next passage represents several new obstacles for the student. This is nearly universally misread and misinterpreted. Let's start with the first bar. The end of the dotted eighth has most likely not been defined, and subsequently, with the rising tension over having to play the dreaded thirty-second-note triplets, causes a missed note a high percentage of the time on the next F! The results become exacerbated in that the end of the tied F has no definition, the printed *piano* dynamic does not occur, the triplet sixteenths are rushed without subdivision, and the G-flat is both incorrectly slurred into the F and undefined (or perhaps slurred) the rest of the bar. At this point, usually another attempt is desired or required to continue. If the student chooses to continue, lack of definition persists with the dotted eighth once again, and the C has no defined end, likely leading to the sixteenths performed without subdivision and the dynamics disregarded completely. As an aside, if the G-flat was played correctly, it likely was not in tune, or related to the F.

Here we illustrate a way to be involved in the process. The first note prepares the second. The end of that note must now be defined, properly preparing the thirty-second-note triplet. The triplet is in a [2,3,1] grouping to avoid over-accenting the downbeat. Another way to notate the dotted eighth ended properly would be to write the eighth note with a sixteenth note tied. If you remove the tie and play the sixteenth, that would illustrate the intent. Since we lowered the F for the purposes of intonation and resonance, we now must take care of the end of the F to define where the second sixteenth-note triplet will begin. Now in triplets to avoid the obvious, and encourage less pogo-stick-like beats, the [2,3,1] grouping is employed. The neglected G-flat should be short, and the F that follows leads to the following decorated F appoggiaturas that resolve to E-flat. We repeat a similar process in the next bar as in bar one, only now paying attention to the end of the C and grouping as indicated with the A lowered, resolving the B-flat minor triad from the lingering C appoggiatura.

As the student continues, maybe they see the G-flat—maybe not—but the inflection is not usually part of a sequence that will go up a half-step in the following bar. Without grouping, the student will run into rhythmic challenges, intonation problems, and a general lack of comprehension. After the sixteenths, the triplets may be too fast and the *ritardando* is disjunct and uncomfortable.

We can now conceptually approach the first tritone section as part of a sequence with confidence and creativity. In this section, we have revisited the C/B-flat appoggiatura in its full glory and resonance. Now a discussion can take place about what strategy one wants to impose for the *ritardando*. We can use our creativity to make the transition from triple to duple by making them equal, achieving the *ritardando* naturally. One could also pretend the first three sixteenths are part of a triplet in metric modulation.

We have reached the *meno* section in a new key. The G-flat may resurface, but has the character dramatically changed? One hopes so! As before, the student may overemphasize the top note, leading to the similar problem of the misplaced downbeat and creating a sort of 2/4 to 4/4. The anxiety ensuing over the impending scale will cause problems as well. The A-flat major scale may surface (D natural is printed); the thirty-seconds rarely begin at the right moment, or are rhythmically inaccurate and rushed beyond recognition. The A-flat eighth note is not preparing the next bar, and the triplets are rushed. The A-flat slur is not observed and the sixteenths that follow are mercilessly rushed. The tie is not defined, and that compounds rhythmical mayhem. Triplets will likely be rushed and pedantic without grouping across the bar line. With the duple/triple groupings lacking, it may lead to inaccuracies and a lack of comprehension in this rendition. The lack of subdivision creates a high probability of mistakes.

If you think about the ends of the notes and subdivide in the provided groupings, the harmony, structure, and rhythm will maintain integrity and the piece will reveal what's necessary. Within that structure is freedom of expression and creativity for variation.

The Theory in Concept, Context, and Practice

Addressing the next passages without grouping results in the likely pulsing on downbeats to the detriment of the phrases, and lack of involvement and engagement that will propel the listener's interest. Additionally, we now have the added challenges of wide intervallic leaps, as well as the responsibility of interpreting the composer's wish to *stringendo* and pace within a longer phrase and to slow later in the form of a *recitative*. Harmonically, the progression becomes even more complex. Without organization, it may be difficult to recognize the semblance of such a sequence as it occurs before the 6/8. A classic mistake is accenting the top notes. *What about this 6/8? Isn't it just the opening again? Why bother to rebar?* It is quite intentional, and understanding comes from the organization he suggests. The novice will not inflect the large "two" feel that is clearly implied.

The groupings in this passage are a virtual testimony to what process-oriented thinking can achieve. If you invest completely in being involved in that, as opposed to the external distractions of the difficulty, you will quickly begin to discover new capabilities in digesting through indirection. You are in the present—not ahead or behind. Everything is organized in the moment. The composer has asked us to perform this in the form of recited words. This organization gives you the freedom to achieve that directive. There are challenges to address specifically. In the wide intervals, experiment with taking the low notes up an octave and then recreating that ease. Pay great attention to the function of the notes in the passage. For instance, when leaping from third-space C to A-flat below the staff, the C should intentionally be lowered to compensate, as it is functioning as the third. Likewise, consider that the leading tone before it in bar four should be lowered. Go ahead and experiment with all the discussed concepts. This passage will teach you more than you thought possible. Pay attention to lower neighbor tones (i.e., where notes come from or lead to), sequences that are less obvious, and enharmonic equivalents. This will all lead you to a path of discovery, experimenting with ways to play differently and with great and complete understanding. In short, you will be free to enjoy and sing what is in your mind. Go ahead and commit to the mindfulness of the end of the note. Right-handed people, tap your left foot (right foot for left-handed)—this will help engage right-brain thinking!

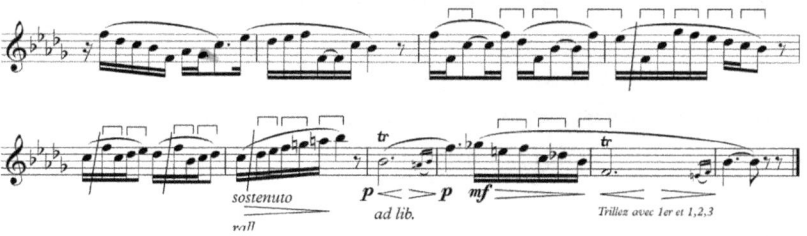

As we come to the close of this etude, here are a few final thoughts. There is, perhaps, a slight decrescendo implied in the *sostenuto*. Additionally, consider using the speed of the trill for the crescendo and reducing the speed for the diminuendo. Don't forget to subdivide eighths throughout the trill and all the way to the grace notes defining the approaching downbeat. Keep in mind that the upper note should be kept lower. Make the interval smaller.

Arban Characteristic Study No. 1*

Before we begin, this seems to be an opportune time to address some confusion about the *gruppetto* (turn). Please refer to the Arban *Complete Conservatory Method* (Goldman/Smith edition), pages 87 and 99–102. Page 87 clearly explains the two different types of gruppetto, and how the shape of the symbol determines whether the turn starts on the upper or lower note. This is followed through in the examples on pages 99–101, with the correct sign for starting on the upper note. But then on page 102, the sign still indicates to begin on the upper note, instead of inverting it to start correctly on the lower note, as all the examples are indicating. Then, to add to the confusion (or simply carelessness), the incorrect sign is used in all of the *Characteristic Studies*. All of the gruppetti should start from the upper note, even though the signs all indicate to start on the lower.

With that out of the way, *Characteristic Study #1* presents many opportunities to apply parts of my theory, including note grouping, articulation, and length of note. As a general rule for note grouping in this etude, subdivide so as to avoid having more than two notes per group, except when playing triplets. This will help keep the tempo much

---

*Conversation transcribed by Daniel Rosenthal, Boston jazz artist

more consistent and give you more anchors or posts to hang your fence on.

When the notes are slurred (such as in the opening measure, Example 1 below) there is a tendency to play them the same length as when they are detached. Especially when playing the lower neighbor, such as in the following phrase, the player will often rush the first two notes, and find themselves increasing the overall tempo more and more.

Example 1
Allegro moderato.

Grouping notes across subdivisions (Example 2, below) helps to both prevent rushing and prevent "pogo-stick phrasing." Also, make sure the "T" is at the end of the note, to give shape to the *detaché* notes. This way, the player doesn't have to worry about tonguing the beginning of the notes as much. When you focus on the end of the note, you cover the beginning and middle of the note as well.

Example 2
Allegro moderato.

With the three slurred sixteenth notes, you have to make the last one short because it's followed by a detached note. It's not necessarily that much shorter, but you have to shape the end of the note with a "T" (dhoT) so that the next note comes out correctly.

Later, putting an accent on the low C (Example 3, below), makes the phrase in measure 11 much more locked in. With across-the-pulse note grouping the G above the staff in the second measure belongs to the E that follows it. Grouping these notes together will help the trumpeter worry less about the wider jump from the C to the G at the beginning of the measure.

Example 3

Now we come to the triplet sixteenth notes (Figure 4).

Example 4

Many students have a tendency to play this phrase almost like two thirty-seconds followed by a sixteenth, because the triplet comes back to the same note that it starts on. You can avoid this by grouping across the pulse (2,3,1, as illustrated in Example 5), keeping the rhythm as even triplets, while maintaining forward momentum in phrasing.

Example 5

In the following measures (Example 6), be careful not to fall into the trap of playing the last sixteenths of the measure (beat four) as triplets; they are duple. Subdividing into eighth notes will alleviate this trap!

Remember that after any tied note, it's important to take a breath. We see that later in Example 7 (below), where the note that comes after the tie belongs to the next pulse.

Later, pay careful attention to ending the D clearly in Example 8, giving shape to the end of the note. The C that follows it belongs to the G on the downbeat of 3.

Pay close attention to the articulations on beat four in Example 9.

These are different than anything we've seen previously in this etude. You have to make the second and fourth sixteenth notes *legato* because the slurs are grouped on the beat. Do not leave space between these and the following notes. This passage is similar in this sense to the "Ballerina Dance" from *Petrouchka*.

I always hear a voice saying, "It's too much overanalyzing." But it's not overanalyzing, it's participating in what you're doing. It also then allows you to play with nuance in between, because there's a tendency to play everything back like a computer: no inflection, no nuance—and we've heard performers do that. That will very likely put the audience to sleep quickly.

In any phrase or group of notes, the most important note is the one of shortest duration. Every note is important, but you have to define the content so the composer can define the context. We're establishing how various notes are played, given the context that they're in, but also following the basic rules of how those notes are played in any situation. If you don't define the content, it doesn't matter what you play: everything is going to sound the same and it becomes like white noise after a while.

In Example 10 above, it's natural to add a crescendo. It's not so much because it needs a crescendo, but more to make sure the energy carries you through the phrase, because it's the first time you've had a dotted eighth slurred to a sixteenth in the piece.

In Example 11 above, it's the second time that you have to slur with the pulse in the piece. Be sure not to play the first D-natural short. It's grouped to the following note, so should be held for its full length. This will keep you from falling into the trap of playing the following dotted sixteenth too short as well.

Example 12

In Example 12 above, avoid the natural acoustic crescendo as you hit the high G by adding a small crescendo during the first half of the phrase and then backing off as you go up to the G. This helps you avoid making the third beat of the measure too strong, making it sound like two 2/4 measures instead of one measure in 4/4. When playing, imagine pushing a ball halfway up a hill and then letting the momentum carry the ball to settle at the top of the hill, rather than pushing it over the hill the entire way.

The biggest gremlin of all that we deal with is complacency. As soon you say, "I know this," or pat yourself on the back, the gremlin sets you up to screw up whatever is coming next. Then, after a mistake is made, you screw up again, because you're busy evaluating the previous mistake. I used to say that if Carl Jung could come back and spend an afternoon in my studio, he'd have all the evidence needed to prove his theory of the "collective unconscious." It's pretty universal for trumpet players. It's not that I'm clairvoyant, but I know where people are going to screw up because I've already been there and done that!

second intermission

BSO Brass and Canadian Brass gather outside the back of the Tanglewood Shed, prior to a 1986 "Brass Bash" concert. Left to right, kneeling, Ron Romm, Chuck Dallenbach, Chester Schmitz, David Ohanian; standing, Doug Yeo, Eugene Watts, Jay Wadenpfuhl, Ron Barron, Charlie Schlueter, André Côme, and Fred Mills. The event was so successful that it was followed two years later with a concert in which the Empire Brass also joined in.

William Vacchiano joined the New York Philharmonic in 1934 as third trumpet/assistant principal with Harry Glantz. He became principal when Glantz went to the NBC Symphony in 1942 and held the position until his retirement in 1973. He also taught at Juilliard from 1935 to 2002. I was fortunate to study with him and hear him perform during his peak years. His sound had such presence, it reached out and touched you. A great musician first who also was a great trumpet player and teacher, Bill knew how to challenge his students to learn how to learn.

I stayed in touch with Bill because I thought about him every time I played an orchestral concert, especially when playing repertoire that I had heard him play. I only had weekly lessons with him for four years, but I continued to learn from him for another 40-plus years. Growing up in Maine, Bill had studied with many teachers because they came to that state on vacation. Every time I talked to him, he would mention one of them or a player I had never heard of, and he would tell me what kind of mouthpiece each played, what his strengths and weaknesses were. Through those stories from Bill, I felt a connection to such luminaries as Herbert Clarke, Max Schlossberg, and three of my predecessors as BSO principal: Louis Kloepfel (1898–1914), Gustav Heim (1914–1919), and Georges Mager (1919–1950).

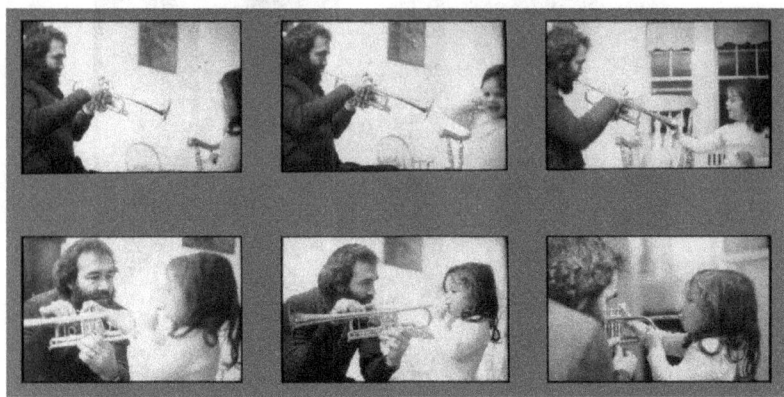

Miriam Fife's first trumpet lesson in February 1981, when I auditioned for principal trumpet of the Boston Symphony Orchestra. Bill Moyers, BSO personnel manager, had called me on a Tuesday inviting me to audition on Thursday of the following week! I told him I couldn't do that but that I could come out to Boston the next day and play on Thursday of that week. I stayed with Miriam's parents and must have sparked Miriam's curiosity, because she took up the trumpet about 10 years later and eventually studied with Seymour Rosenfeld of the Philadelphia Orchestra.

second intermission

Though he was sick with the flu on what was his 29th birthday, Wynton joined me in 1990 when we each received a first prototype of Monette's Raja models; his, #825, was a B-flat, and mine, #822, was a C.

Taken the same day as the photo above.

Sailing around Boston Harbor, circa early 2000s. My friend Bob Olson, a BSO bass player, had a 30-foot sailboat that he docked in Winthrop on Boston's north shore. I sold my own 23-foot sloop before I left Minneapolis. Though I grew up in a mining town, as an adult I always loved being near water, whether in my Plum Island cottage within sight of the Atlantic Ocean or, later, our Lenox summer place uphill from the Stockbridge Bowl.

Backstage after a performance of Bach's B-minor Mass in Westerly, Rhode Island in 1985; with Tom Crown (left) and Ed Tarr. This was not a BSO gig. George Kent, an organist and trumpet player, also conducted at a church in Westerly. He had engaged Ed to play first and asked me if I would mind playing second. Why not? I loved concerts like this, with an opportunity to perform a great work in a place where such a concert might be the musical highlight of the community's year.

With my great friend of half a century, Doc Severinsen.

Teaching a master class in Brazil in 2018.

Part III
Principles of the Process

Breathing

Posture

Posture is the quintessential aspect of breathing efficiently. Practicing the Alexander Technique, Feldenkrais' Awareness Through Movement®, or yoga will be extremely beneficial in developing proper posture. David Monette has provided a very helpful summation of efficient posture at his website, www.monette.net.

Standing

When standing, if the hips are forward and the body is arched, the hips are blocked and the player cuts the torso off from the legs and feet. The muscle tension in the legs and torso caused by this misalignment greatly inhibits a player's ability to take in a full, relaxed breath. This will result in playing high on the pitch.

The center of the ear should be over the center of the shoulder, which should be over the waist, which should be over the ankle. With this alignment, the skeletal structure can hold up most of the body's weight, allowing the player to stay more open and breathe much more freely. This allows the player to play with their entire body. In Hatha yoga, this is called "Mountain Pose." This posture will allow one to play down into the center of the pitch.

To assume this position, stand with your feet parallel and shoulder width apart. Move your hips backward and forward, and notice the change in weight distribution. When the hips are forward, the body weight is on the balls of the feet and/or toes. When the hips are back, the body weight is more on the heels.

Find the position where your body weight is evenly distributed front to back and side to side on your feet, then unlock your knees. This is the most efficient and aligned way to stand. This simple shift in standing may make you feel like you are falling forward slightly, compared to how you are used to standing. You may also be uncomfortable standing with your feet parallel rather than splayed. If, however, you concentrate on your feet, legs, and breath with this new approach, you will notice you feel more solid and grounded as you stand, and your breath will be freer and much more open.

Sitting

If one's sitting head is forward of the spine, and the back of the neck is compressed, the throat is blocked, inhibiting the breath and killing the natural resonance of the player. This will result in playing high on the pitch. Also note that if the feet are splayed and legs extended (which blocks the hips and closes off even more of the body), the player will be forced even higher above the optimum pitch center.

When the head is over the spine and the back of the neck is extended, the throat remains open. When the feet are parallel and the lower legs are vertical, allowing the hips to open, one can play down into the center of the pitch—open, aligned, and centered.

Air is the raw material out of which tone is created. Therefore, the primary components of playing the trumpet are breathing and how the air is used. Before the air can be used, it must be available. Thus, inhaling is the most important aspect of breathing. To expel the air and create a tone, the lungs must first be filled.

Misunderstanding

There is probably more *misunderstanding, misconception,* and *misinformation* about breathing than about any other subject pertaining to trumpet playing. In 1950, three years before I got to high school, Mel Siener, the newly arrived band director at the high school, gave me a brand-new copy of J. B. Arban's *Complete Conservatory Method* (edited by Edwin Franko Goldman and Walter M. Smith), copyright 1938. It was the only copy of the Arban book I ever owned.

In the section entitled Method of Breathing, Arban explains: "The mouthpiece having been placed on the lips, the mouth should partly open at the sides, and the tongue retire, in order to allow the air to penetrate into the lungs. The stomach ought not to swell, but, on the contrary, rather recede, in proportion as the chest is dilated by the respiration." In a footnote, the editors add: "The diaphragmatic system of breathing, almost universally used at the present time, teaches the drawing of the breath directly to the diaphragm, which causes a slight distention of the body about the waistline. More complete control, greater power, and more ease in the upper register, with a noticeable lessening of pressure on the lips, are the advantages to be gained by this system."

There are many misunderstandings about diaphragmatic breathing. Most importantly, it is impossible to breathe without the diaphragm! If some injury should occur to one's diaphragm so that it would not function, that person would die if not immediately placed on some sort of artificial respiratory device. The diaphragm is one of the involuntary muscles in the body—the only time one is even aware that one has a diaphragm is when it is functioning abnormally, specifically when suffering from the hiccoughs (hiccups), where the diaphragm is going up when it should be going down. What are some of the suggested cures for hiccoughs? The most common include holding your breath while counting to 10, taking nine sips of water, breathing into and out of a paper bag, and startling the person who is hiccoughing. All of these solutions are supposed to help get the diaphragm back in sync; that is, moving down when inhaling, and back up when exhaling (what it is supposed to do involuntarily).

Whether one is lying down or sitting in a chair breathing "normally," the abdomen (stomach) expands when inhaling and retracts when exhaling. Consequently, many trumpet players conclude that this action needs only to be exaggerated to play the trumpet efficiently. Since the diaphragm does flatten downward when inhaling, and the thorax rests on the diaphragm area due to gravity when one is sitting or standing, abdominal expansion is from the internal organs being pushed downward (and outward) by the descending diaphragm, which occurs because there is less resistance to expansion below the rib cage. This is *not* an indication that the lungs are being filled completely. Additionally, filling the lungs to the maximum capacity does not necessitate expanding the abdomen. The diaphragm is attached to the lower ribs. If the lower ribs are expanded as the diaphragm moves down, then the abdomen will not protrude.

Misconceptions

There are many misconceptions about breathing:

Taking in too much air will cause hyperventilation. Hyperventilation is breathing too rapidly and shallowly.

In reality, hyperventilation causes the body to get rid of too much carbon dioxide; it does not result in too much oxygen.

Taking in too much air will cause tension. If tightness is experienced when inhaling to the maximum, it means there is too much tightness (tension), not too much air.

Taking in too much air will make you dizzy. Tension, not tightness, can cause dizziness.

One needs to "support" the air by voluntary muscle action (diaphragm support). The diaphragm is a muscle of inhalation, not exhalation. Therefore, the diaphragm does not "support" the air; it is not responsible for expelling the air.

Chest expansion indicates shallow breathing. The lungs are inside the rib cage (chest).

Abdominal expansion indicates deep breathing. Not necessarily! The diaphragm does move downward when inhaling, as it is attached to the bottom ribs. Therefore, the bottom of the rib cage should move outward (see above).

Misinformation

There are many maxims on breathing that I have found to be misinformed and counterproductive. Among them:

- Only take in the amount of air you need.
- Use all of your air before taking another breath.
- Don't let the chest expand; it will make you tight.
- Get rid of stale air.
- Don't inhale too soon.

It has been my experience, through playing as well as teaching, that nearly all musical and technical problems are really symptoms of insufficient or poor breathing.

Most difficulties arise when the initial inhalation is of insufficient volume and the player is left with insufficient air available for playing. Although some of the problems caused by insufficient quantity of air are obvious, many are not. The following is a more or less complete checklist (in alphabetical order) of areas in which problems can arise from poor or insufficient breathing:

- anxiety
- articulation: slurring, tonguing
- dynamic range
- embouchure
- endurance
- flexibility
- intonation
- phrasing
- projection
- range (upper and lower)
- resonance
- response
- technique
- tension/tightness
- timbre
- tone

There is a direct correlation between the volume of air in the lungs and air velocity (how fast the air is expelled). The less air in the lungs, the faster the air must move to produce a sound, because more effort will be required to expel the air. Conversely, the more completely the lungs are filled, the slower the expulsion of air can be.

Often, more emphasis is placed on blowing or expelling the air. One is told to fill the instrument, blow through the instrument, and support the air using the diaphragm or abdominal muscles. This usually results in excessive tension or tightness and further inhibits inhaling to the maximum on subsequent breaths.

Avoiding the Panic Zone

The line graphs below represent the entire range of playing the trumpet, from left (relaxed) to right (tense). The right side, labeled "Panic Zone" is the extreme way of getting the note out by any means: pressure, pinching, squeezing, total tension with no air, panic. The left side illustrates the relative effort involved between inhaling and exhaling. It takes the combined relative effort of inhaling and exhaling to equal 10, although these numbers are an abstract concept in regard to effort—there is no way of actually measuring. The "Inhale" effort is conscious, or mental, and will represent relaxing. More effort spent on inhaling will result in more air available. The "Exhale" effort is physical and represents tightening.

The first graph illustrates the extreme case of zero effort involved in inhaling (consequently no air), and the maximum effort of 10 to exhale (or expel) whatever residual air is in the lungs. Here are two examples: (1) If a young child wants to "blow the trumpet" but isn't told to "take a breath," they will blow, and if a sound is produced at all, it will not be a very nice sound. (2) When a trumpet player attempts to play the first technical study by Herbert L. Clarke, 8–16 repetitions in one breath (assuming "a big breath" was taken), when nearing the end of the lungs' air supply, more and more effort is required (blowing harder, resulting in more velocity) to get that air out to make a sound (effort of 10). The last sound they can make will not be much better than the one a young child produces with no inhalation.

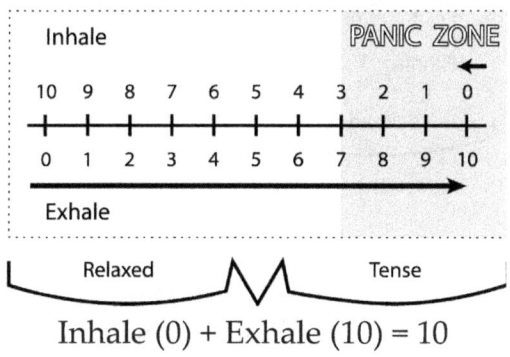

Inhale (0) + Exhale (10) = 10

The second graph (below) illustrates an inhale effort of 6 (which represents 60% capacity), and an exhale effort of 4. As soon as one starts playing (blowing), the volume of air decreases and the effort to get the air out increases until it reaches 10, or 0% capacity.

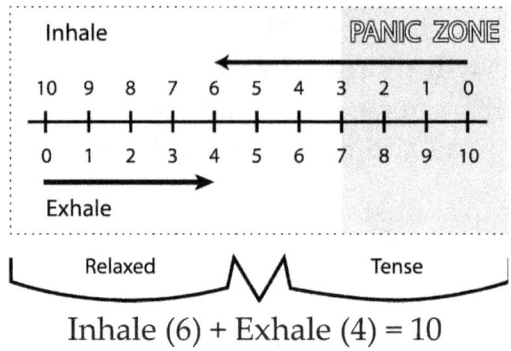

Inhale (6) + Exhale (4) = 10

The third graph illustrates an inhale effort of 10 (which represents 100% capacity), and an exhale effort of 0. Ideally, one should not go past an exhale effort of 5 before inhaling again. When exhaling to an effort of 10, the size of the container (the lungs) has been reduced (and the muscles tightened), and it will take even greater effort to fill to capacity (maximum).

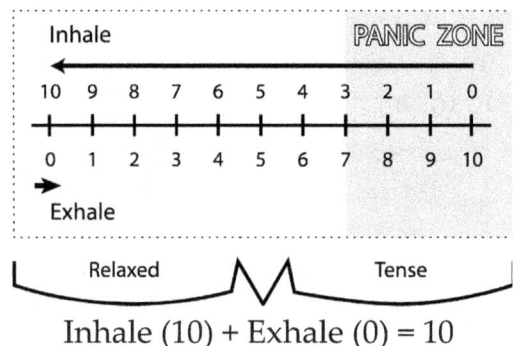

Inhale (10) + Exhale (0) = 10

The advice to take in only the amount of air needed implies one should inhale the amount of air necessary to play a particular phrase. What is not considered is that to create the kind of tone desired or required, the air must be set into vibration at the appropriate frequency in the same length of tubing. Insufficient air supply will cause inefficient use of the air. In addition to having enough air to produce a tone or phrase, one must also supply one's body (particularly the brain) with enough air to function. Additionally, if the player only inhales according to what's to be played, they become locked into playing that phrase exactly the same way without any gradations in dynamic, color, tempo, or nuance. If the available volume of air is insufficient, velocity will become the means for producing a tone. This severely limits the range of dynamics and timbre.

How does one achieve the maximum inhalation? There are various ways to achieve this. One way is to say "Ho" when taking a breath. This is facilitated by making a circle with the thumb and forefinger about the size of a nickel. Pull the air through this opening. This is the starting point—when you have taken in as much as you think you can, put your lips together as if you were going to play, and take small sips. The lips create resistance and the air should sting your tongue. Continue sipping—if you open your lips, the resistance will shift to your throat and it will feel like you are "bottled up." As long as the lips are together, the abdomen will stay soft; so as long as you keep your lips tight together, you will be able to continue sipping! While sipping, bring the trumpet up to your lips, then play second line G. If you have enough air, the note will speak like someone else did it for you (zero effort, as in the chart above). If it doesn't, continue to sip; do not expel the air in your lungs or you will have to start over. Take a few more sips and try the G again—*mp* or less. Think hot air! This routine is primarily done during the first playing of the day. After you get the note to speak, then you can exhale. Inhale again, trying to reach the volume you had after sipping.

Only humans are capable of producing either hot or cold air, depending on what is desired, as well as of controlling the speed of the air we exhale: hot air if we have cold hands; cold air to cool a hot liquid. Consequently, thinking of using warm air is conducive to creating a sound of maximum resonance. If you are even aware of your mouth, it means there is insufficient air in your lungs!

Tone and Resonance

In order to achieve high quality tone, one must strive for maximum resonance. Maximum resonance means the tone contains as many overtones as are acoustically possible. The instrument must be played where it wants to be played, that is, where it best resonates. I will use some drawings to help demonstrate what I mean. They will not necessarily be totally to scale according to the laws of physics, but I hope they will help to clarify the concept. All the overtones must be in tune with each other and with the principal note. To find where the trumpet wants to be played, proceed as follows (on a B-flat trumpet):

- While pressing the second valve, tap on the mouthpiece with your flattened palm. This will produce a resonating pop of concert A.
- If necessary, adjust the tuning slide so that the pop is in tune.
- Play either low or middle B, check the pop again. Make sure you are playing at the same pitch as the pop.

It is at this point the instrument wants to be played. One must then play the entire range of the trumpet using this concept.

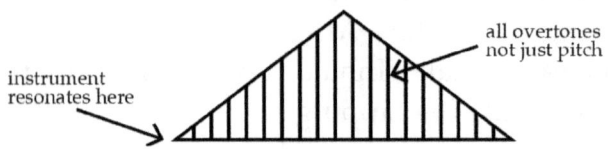

If tuned in this way, the instrument will be in tune with itself and be capable of maximum resonance. It will be in focus. I prefer the concept of focusing rather than centering, because centering implies aiming at the middle of the note, which is not what we are looking for here.

Why use the image of a triangle here? This helps to visualize how the centering approach would considerably reduce the resonance of the tone: by centering, one is eliminating the lower overtones, and therefore one produces a smaller, brighter, and all too often even a pinched or at least a thin tone. If you think of centering as aiming at the middle or center of the tone, like a bull's-eye, the player will end up creating a bottom line that eliminates the lower frequencies and the resulting tone will be thin, bright, edgy, and most likely sound out of tune (thus making it difficult to play in tune with other players).

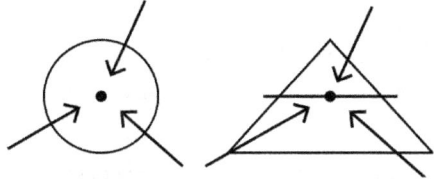

If, however, the player thinks of the center as being the broadest or widest or thickest part of the sound, then the player is more likely to play with maximum resonance—the complete palette—the "sweet spot" of the tone.

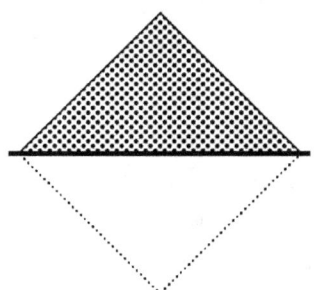

I find that it can also be helpful to visualize tone as a three-dimensional object.

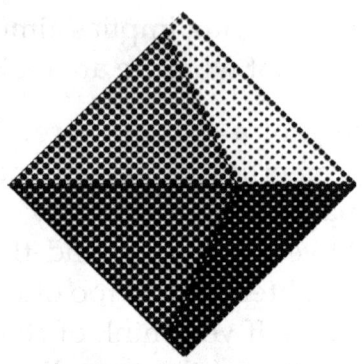

It is often believed that a bright tone (one that has no fundamental in the sound, only the higher frequencies) projects better than a dark tone (one in which the lower frequencies dominate). It has been my experience that the opposite is true—because of the construction of the trumpet and the trumpet mouthpiece, higher frequencies are generally more prominent than they are in the tone of a cornet or flugelhorn. That makes it all the more important for the trumpet player to strive for the maximum resonance (lower frequencies) as the lower frequencies (larger sound waves) carry the higher frequencies, resulting in maximum projection. It is also, of course, critical to remember that minimum intensity (using slow air, as explained in the breathing section above) is central to achieving maximum resonance.

Intonation

The trumpet has inherent intonation problems, regardless of the manufacturer. That's just the nature of the beast; however, many trumpets have many intonation problems beyond the inherent ones. And many intonation problems are the fault of the mouthpiece.

As is obvious, the modern piston trumpet is a combination of seven trumpets (i.e., one for each valve combination: open (0), 2, 1, 1-2, 2-3, 1-3, 1-2-3). The main problem is the second valve; this is the half-step valve.

Let us go through an example, assuming that the open overtone series is on a C trumpet. Any note on the open overtone series (C, G, C, E, G, C) will be lowered one half-step by depressing the second valve, which adds approximately two inches of tubing to the approximately four feet of open length (resulting in B, F-sharp, B, D-sharp, F-sharp, B). Now, this is not where the problem of the second valve manifests. In fact, up to this point, the pitch (intonation) of the second valve is still okay, as long as the three different notes serve as a tonic of a major or minor tonality.

The problem shows up after the first valve is depressed. This action lowers the open overtones one whole step (i.e., two half-steps) by adding approximately four inches—or twice the length of the second valve alone—to the overall length (now B-flat, F, B-flat, D, F, B-flat). Adding the second valve to lower the first valve by one half-step leads to an often neglected problem: the second valve tubing is no longer one half-step, since the instrument is now another of the seven trumpets, that is, it is not, strictly speaking, a C trumpet anymore. Once the first valve has been depressed, it is a B-flat trumpet.

Thus, all notes played with the first and second valves (A, E, A, C-sharp, A, C-sharp) are too sharp (even when any of these happen to be a tonic). And this problem continues as we lengthen the overall tubing.

Although the third valve produces the same overtones as the first plus second on practically every trumpet, regardless of pitch (key) or manufacturer, the third valve notes are, nevertheless, slightly lower in pitch. In spite of this, when we add the second valve to it—to play A-flat, E-flat, etc.—this combination will still be too sharp.

Once we move to 1-3 and 1-2-3 combinations, things will get even worse. These, as everyone knows, are very sharp and need to be lowered by extending the third slide (preferably), or a combination of both first and third slides, for the same reasons.

If the intonation of these notes is not corrected with the slide(s), the alternative is to "lip down" these notes, or to play them where they are. In the latter case, the succeeding notes will then be played too high. By not mechanically adjusting the slides, the player will inadvertently end up playing the rest of the instrument too high.

Although the above example was based on a C trumpet, similar intonation discrepancies occur on all of the other trumpets: D, E-flat, F, G, piccolo in A/B-flat, and, of course, B-flat trumpet (on which everyone first learns to play).

The problem of faulty intonation first occurs when a beginner is learning to play on a student instrument (without slide rings, saddles, or triggers), and/or when playing in a band where, very often, intonation is not a high priority, and these necessary adjustments are ignored.

It has only been in the last 40–45 years that even professional instruments have started to come equipped with first-slide tuning devices. Therefore, many players have assumed that first slide, and sometimes even third slide, adjustments were unnecessary.

The first time a C major scale is played without lowering the first line E and second space A (and even worse, without lowering the D below the staff), the student is beginning to learn faulty intonation (as well as creating future problems with embouchure, range, endurance, articulation, tone, etc.). In this case, the E and the A must be lowered further still because each is the major third of the tonic and subdominant chords, respectively. The leading tone is actually the major third of the dominant chord and therefore must be lowered also.

The only time the first slide is not pulled when playing a note with first and second valves is when that note is the third of a minor chord (e.g., when playing the opening of Mahler 5 on a C trumpet, the first line E and the second space A are the minor thirds of C-sharp minor and F-sharp minor, respectively).

How far must the first and third slides be pulled? For a C major scale on a B-flat trumpet: for the D below the staff, the third slide needs to be taken out about three-quarters of an inch; for the first line E (third of the C major chord) and the second space A (third of the F major chord), the first slide should be pulled out about one-quarter of an inch (this is about one-eighth of an inch further than if each were the tonic of their respective keys of E major/minor and A major/minor). The first slide will be back in for F and open G. For the A, the first slide will be out approximately one-quarter of an inch because this is the third of the subdominant (similarly, the first slide will be out about one-eighth of an inch further than if the A were the tonic of A major).

Many so-called "technical" difficulties players encounter are partly related to faulty intonation in their playing. Take, for example, Clarke's *Technical Studies*. If the first and third slides are not used on the notes below the staff in the first five or six exercises of each study, the notes that are too sharp either will have to be "lipped" down, or the notes that are okay will end up being "lipped" up to match the out-of-tune notes, thus making the whole instrument too sharp. A chromatic scale must be treated as a modified diatonic major scale. In the first study, for instance, although the notes are chromatic, the mediant (i.e., the third degree of the major scale) must be lowered approximately 14 cents (one cent = 1/100 of a semitone).

Question: How useful is it for a trumpet player to check their intonation on a piece by referring some notes to a piano?

The only intervals you can check with the piano are octaves or unisons—and even then, only notes that are tonics. Since the piano is tuned to "tempered pitch," it is really "out of tune." Unfortunately, ear training is usually done with a keyboard instrument. Therefore, we have another problem: we are trained to hear intonation that produces a handicap when we play a non-tempered instrument.

If you want to tune each note of a trumpet with a piano, each is only valid if the twelve notes are tonic.

For further information on just intonation, see the chart on pages 222–223, as well as the works of Christopher Leuba and Jack Holland.

Embouchure

Since the lips are the point of contact with the instrument, a great deal of attention is focused on the embouchure. In music, the embouchure describes a complex relationship between the lips and the mouthpiece. Very often, the embouchure gets the credit when everything works and the blame when it doesn't (great chops, lousy chops, etc.). In most cases, this emphasis is misplaced.

If the embouchure were of prime importance, then there are many trumpet players who should not have been able to play at all, based on how their embouchure "looks," but who are revered as some of the greatest players.

First, there is nothing "natural" about playing the trumpet—though this could be said about playing any instrument.

No two people have the same lip and/or dental structure. There are thin lips and thick lips; large teeth and small teeth; straight teeth and crooked teeth; and everything in between. In the United States especially, much money is paid to orthodontists to have the teeth straightened—even when trumpet playing isn't being considered. Having straight, even teeth doesn't mean that the "embouchure" will function any better. I have observed trumpet players in other countries who either don't have the means or the opportunity to have the work done on their teeth (players who have extra-large teeth, extra teeth, crooked teeth) who somehow manage to play very well.

However, there is a certain similarity in their lip structure, and that is their lower lip is usually thicker (therefore the muscles are larger) than the upper.

There are many theories about how the mouthpiece should be placed on the lips: half on upper, half on lower;

one-third upper, two-thirds lower; two-thirds upper, one-third lower. There is probably general agreement that the mouthpiece should be placed in the center of the mouth (although that is difficult to measure), but there have been many players who have placed the mouthpiece more to one side or the other, and even some extreme off-center cases, but, nevertheless, these players have been successful. That said, however, I tend to agree with Arban that the mouthpiece ought to be placed one-third on the upper lip and two-thirds on the lower, or at least more of the mouthpiece on the lower lip because, as stated before, the lower lip is bigger, having more muscle.

It has been stated that the upper (top) lip is the more important and that only the upper lip vibrates. If that were the case, then it wouldn't matter where the mouthpiece was placed (if at all) on the lower lip. There is a tendency for the upper lip to curl out in the middle. When simply placing the mouthpiece on the lips (regardless of the proportion), and no matter what shape or size of the rim, both lips will tend to "roll out," even without undue pressure. As soon as the air starts to move, it will add to this tendency. If there is insufficient air available, resulting in more velocity, this problem will be exaggerated. This often leads to excessive pressure. When the lips get injured, it is almost always the top lip that gets hurt as a result of excessive pressure.

The lower lip, attached to the movable part of the face (the jaw), has a tendency to get out of the way if too much pressure is applied, leaving the upper lip to take the brunt of whatever pressure there is (there have been players who have advocated non-pressure, but I have never met one). Excessive pressure is a result of insufficient air, which causes the abdominal muscles to contract (tighten) too much. This tension then travels up the back and down the arms—resulting in too much pressure on the lips!

Although non-pressure may not be practical (or entirely possible), one should strive to use minimal pressure. By using more of the lower lip, that lip will be able to tolerate more of the weight of the mouthpiece. My experience is that the lower lip is more responsible for range, endurance, flexibility, articulation, and intonation. But again, an insufficient volume of air will cause all of the muscles to tighten more than is necessary, resulting in too much pressure. One of the many paradoxes in trumpet playing is that as the muscles and lips become stronger, they also lose sensitivity. This can lead to pressure creeping into one's playing and, ultimately, injury if the player is not vigilant in minimizing pressure.

Always inhaling to the maximum is more conducive to avoiding muscle tension while playing the trumpet. Also, keep in mind that it is necessary to provide the brain with the oxygen it needs to function at maximum efficiency — we need air for that as well as for the raw material to make beautiful music.

If one is going to build a house or a piece of furniture, the prerequisites would be a concept (a set of plans) and an excellent set of tools: saws, hammers, screwdrivers, planes, sandpaper, nails, screws, paint and/or varnish, etc. But most importantly, one needs the raw material: wood. And it is necessary to buy more than the "required" amount of wood — there will always be waste (sawdust and scraps). Likewise, in trumpet playing, the prerequisites would be the concept/set of plans (music), the tools (instrument, mouthpiece), the ear, the lips/embouchure, and technique — articulation, tonguing, slurring, phrasing, nuance, vibrato, dynamics, timbre, etc. But without the raw material — air — none of the above can be used to make any kind of music. First and foremost, the trumpet is a *wind* instrument.

Also, for cooking or baking, one needs a concept, that is, a recipe, and the appropriate utensils for measuring: pots or pans, appropriate spoons and/or mixer. Without the necessary ingredients—raw material—even if one has the tools, one can't make anything.

There are various teaching theories about "buzzing" the lips and/or "buzzing" on the mouthpiece. The most extreme case that I know of is of a teacher in New York (and there are probably still some of his followers) who actually taught the "buzz" system. One of his students could "buzz" from a pedal C to a double high C with his lips on just a mouthpiece (any size) or on the leadpipe (without a mouthpiece). The only problem is that when he actually played on the instrument (with mouthpiece), it sounded like an amplified "buzz." Not much range of timbre there! "Buzzing" on the mouthpiece alone can have some benefits, such as helping to develop the ear, but it doesn't do much for developing a concept of tone. This buzzing practice places the emphasis solely on the air making the lips vibrate, or "buzz."

The function of the lips is to make the air in the instrument vibrate. When a note doesn't speak, the usual interpretation is that the lips are stiff or not vibrating. What is really happening is that the air is moving too fast (too much velocity) and blows the lips apart so they can't make the air in the instrument produce the sound desired. This, again, is from insufficient air in the lungs, leading to too much tension or tightness in the lungs and chest. The lips can only function in relation to what the air is doing. If velocity is used for production instead of for adding intensity or brilliance, it puts an additional burden on the lips. If the lips make the necessary adjustment to compensate for what isn't working efficiently, the desired note will come out; if not, it won't.

To reiterate, the primary function of the lips is to make the air in the trumpet vibrate at the appropriate frequency. The beginning player figures out what to do with their lips to produce a particular note, whether a low C, a G, or a middle C, etc., on the open tones. This, of course, is predicated on the internal "ear" hearing the correct pitch. I don't know of anyone who can describe exactly what the lips must do to achieve that.

So, the most basic concept (how the note is shaped) of trumpet playing is playing the appropriate note (correct overtone or partial). It is a good start. Unfortunately, playing the "correct" pitch is only one part of the whole. The conceptual process must then be developed (or enhanced) to include all of the music!

This is where imagination comes into use. There is not just one way to play anything. If one is playing already-composed music, those notes are the "plan." The player then must play the written notes, rhythms, dynamics, tempo, and style indicated by the composer. But that is only the beginning; phrasing, nuance, expression are supplied by the performer. Although it may be possible to play the passage exactly the same every time (accuracy), why would we want to do that? It would be mechanical and boring—for the performer and for the listener.

Tonguing

What is the function of the tongue in trumpet playing?

The usual answer is to produce the attack of a note. I don't like the word "attack" because of its connotation of violence or aggression.

In his *Complete Conservatory Method*, J. B. Arban uses the expression "commencing" the sound. I prefer this to "attack." He then says, "The tongue should then advance against the teeth of the upper jaw in such a way as to hermetically seal the mouth, as though it were a valve intended to keep the column of air in the lungs." This position is accomplished by thinking of the syllable *tu*. Here is where something got lost in translation. *Tu* is not the same in French as it is in English.

In my experience, I have found that most trumpet players tend to use the tip of the tongue to touch behind the upper teeth, either on the edge, at the gum line, or even further back. It is not possible to "hermetically seal the mouth" by using the tip of the tongue. The tongue can only act as a leaky valve if used in this manner.

In his *Characteristic Studies*, Herbert L. Clarke states: "My tongue is never rigid when playing, and rests at the bottom of my mouth. I then produce the staccato, by the center of the tongue striking against the roof of my mouth." I think this probably comes closer to what I do. The tip of my tongue touches the gum line of the lower teeth and the broadest part of the tongue then touches the back of the upper teeth and gums. I do not—repeat, do not—anchor the tip of the tongue behind the lower teeth. The tongue then will "hermetically seal the mouth" by acting "as a valve."

It is not necessary to depend on the tongue for "commencing the tone." In the section on embouchure, the concept of having the lips make the air in the instrument vibrate—rather than the air making the lips vibrate—was proposed. If that approach is used, then the tone can and will begin without the use of the tongue. Since I said I don't like the term "attack," neither do I think of this as a "breath attack," although that term is often used by players who have developed the courage to start a note without the tongue.

What I propose next is what most trumpet players have been told at one time or another is the ultimate "NO-NO!" I do use my tongue to shape the end of the note, although it is often called "tongue stopping." The advice usually given is, "Don't ever, ever, ever, ever stop a note with your tongue!!!!" If the tongue doesn't shape or define (or stop) a note, then the throat will. The shape of a note is determined by the end of it. Now for a qualifier: I did not say I stop every note I play with my tongue. It would seem obvious that for any note that is of a quarter or more in duration, it is possible to shape the end or release of the note without the tongue's involvement; but for any note shorter than a quarter note (eighth, sixteenth, or thirty-second) to have an exact release (or shape), the use of the tongue is mandatory. Using the tongue in this manner is predicated on the tongue position described above (I have heard that this position is called *dorsal tonguing*). Those who advise against stopping a note with the tongue will also advise to keep the throat open. It is not possible to have it both ways.

Some will say it's okay to use the tongue to stop a note if one is playing jazz, but not if one is playing orchestral or classical music. I say it's a matter of determining how the end of the note is to sound.

The tongue is the valve that determines the end of a note—usually of a shorter duration—but it definitely defines the shape.

The following exercise will be used for showing and learning the relationship between shape, duration, tempo, resonance, and intonation, and how to integrate them:

100 Indirection

This must be played three ways, as follows:

1) Play very slowly, counting in eight (8/8-eighth note pulse) at about a *mf* (not too loud or too soft). The length of the eighths will seem like quarters. The silence connecting them will seem almost nonexistent. The end of one note is the beginning of the next (or, after the first note, the beginning of each succeeding note will be the end of the previous).

The whole note is the gauge (or template) to tell you if the pitch and resonance of the previous eighths were okay. Players tend to use too much velocity when tonguing; remember to inhale to the maximum (cf. "Breathing"); the lips are making the air in the instrument vibrate (cf. "Embouchure"); the tongue is a valve (see above). Be sure to hold the whole note for eight beats (this will partially fulfill the "long tone need"). Inhale to the maximum after each whole note. If endurance becomes an issue, it is a sign of insufficient inhalation.

2) Play at the same tempo, but this time play the eighths as short as possible (even shorter than possible!!). Silence still connects the eighths but is much more obvious than

in the first way. It is very important to concentrate on the ends of the notes. The shortness and use of the tongue as a valve will add rhythmic and articulation energy to the notes, making them louder than before (the first way). Think of hotter, slower air flow, so the overall dynamic is still very close to the first way (*mf*). The whole note is still the gauge for pitch and resonance. As before, the lips are making the air in the instrument vibrate. Inhale to the maximum. Do not rely too much on velocity or the tongue for the beginning of the note—only the end. Make sure all the eighths are the same pitch and resonance and at the same steady pulse.

3) Start at the previous tempo, and begin to accelerate by reducing the silence connecting the notes. **The shape of the notes must stay the same.** Switch to a quarter note pulse as speed increases, and even gradually to half note pulse (*alla breve*). Only the tempo and the silence connecting the eighth notes (and the duration of the whole notes) change. It is necessary to accelerate until the silence connecting the eighth notes is the same as when the length was like quarter notes, that is, the end of one note is the beginning of the next, and vice versa.

In the second and third ways of playing, the shape of the eighth notes is identical. The resonance and dynamic should be the same. It may be necessary to think of making the air flow still hotter and slower. Still, remember to inhale after each whole note. Just because the faster tempo may make it possible to play more notes without inhaling, DON'T!!! It is even more necessary to inhale the maximum amount to ensure maximum concentration and to avoid panic. The focus should still be on the **shape** of the notes, not on tonguing faster.

Six different **shapes** (note values) have just been achieved. In example <u>one</u>, because of the extremely slow tempo, the printed eighths were really (1) quarters; and the printed whole notes were really (2) breves (double whole notes). In example two, the shape of printed (3) eighths was established (albeit extremely secco). And in example three, the shape of eighth notes evolved into the shape of (4) sixteenth notes by the end because of the tempo, and the reduction of the silence connecting them. The shape of (5) whole notes was achieved when the pulse became quarter notes, and (6) half notes were defined by the time the tempo accelerated to *alla breve*.

Note: The shape of eighths and sixteenths is accomplished by the same tongue motion.

The following is from William Vacchiano:

Repeat ad nauseum, then descend chromatically: 2-1-12-23-13-123.

Transposition by Clef

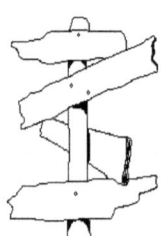

Learning transposition is often one of the most challenging, intimidating, and frustrating requirements of trumpet playing. There are two basic methods of transposition: interval and clef. After about ten minimally successful years of attempting transposition by interval, I finally decided to use clefs. After all, looking at a note in treble clef and calling it by a different name is, essentially, reading another clef.

It should be noted that the use of the term *clef* is somewhat inaccurate in this discussion. There are three clefs: F clef, C clef, and G clef. Generally, the F clef is referred to as the bass clef, the G clef as the treble clef, and the C clef as either the alto clef or the tenor clef (the location of "C" on either the third or the fourth line differentiates alto and tenor clef). Technically, the terms *bass staff, treble staff,* and either *alto* or *tenor staff* should be employed. However, for the purposes of this discussion, the terms may be interchanged.

The great staff has eleven lines:

Incidentally, the word *solfège* derives from sol-fa: sol is the bottom line of the great staff; fa is the top line; "middle C" is the middle line. The shape of the clef signs actually evolved out of their respective letters.

Visualizing the different clefs on the great staff somewhat facilitates learning them.

| Bass | Baritone | Tenor | Alto | Mezzo-Soprano | Soprano | Treble | French-violin |

The names of the various staffs (clefs) [those lines within the boxes above] originated from the normal voice range. Without the context of the great staff, they appear as follows:

By altering the clef sign, the name of any line or space may be changed to any one of seven possibilities:

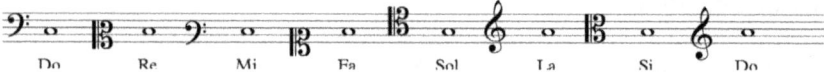

The basic approach of transposition by clef has its origins in the history of orchestral trumpet playing. Before the invention of the modern valved instrument, the trumpet could only play the notes in the natural overtone series. Consequently, orchestral music was always notated in C major and the player's choice of crook determined the transposition. Similarly, modern players approach transposition as if the part were in C major, substitute the appropriate clef, and alter the appropriate accidentals. In this way, the proper notes may be obtained on whatever pitch trumpet we choose.

Because most players in the United States begin on a B-flat trumpet and learn to transpose using that instrument, the following rules for clef transposition apply to the B-flat trumpet. Obviously, if a differently pitched trumpet is used, the appropriate clef should be substituted accordingly.

A-flat trumpet

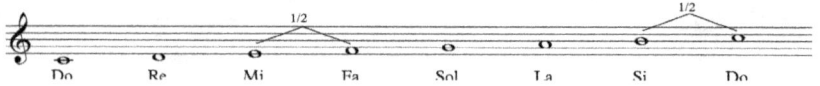

Clef substitution: tenor

Accidentals: lower all ½ step before Si and Mi (in tenor clef)

A trumpet

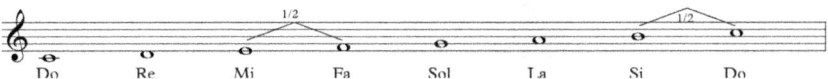

Clef substitution: tenor

Accidentals: raise all ½ step before Fa, Do, Sol, Re, and La (in tenor clef)

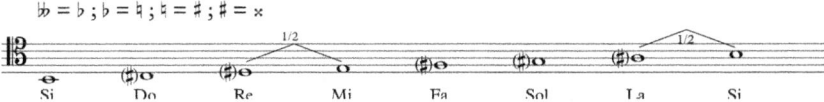

B-natural trumpet (H)

Clef substitution: none (retain treble clef)

Accidentals: raise all ½ step before all notes

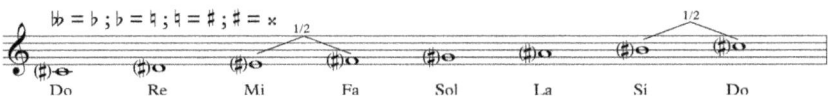

Or, Clef substitution: alto

Accidentals: lower all ½ step before Si, Mi, La, Re and Sol (in alto clef)

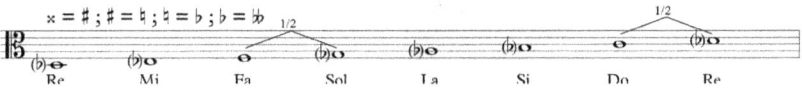

C trumpet

Clef substitution: alto

Accidentals: Raise all ½ step before Fa and Do (in alto clef)

D-flat trumpet

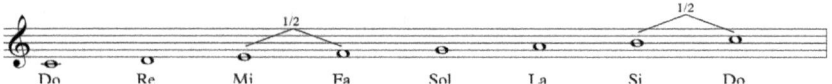

Clef substitution: bass

Accidentals: lower all ½ step before Si, Mi and La (in bass clef)

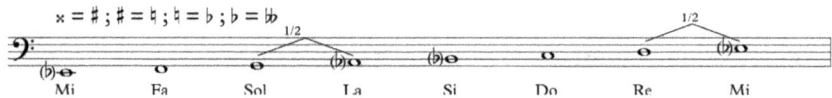

D trumpet

Clef substitution: bass

Accidentals: raise all ½ step before Fa, Do, Sol and Re (in bass clef)

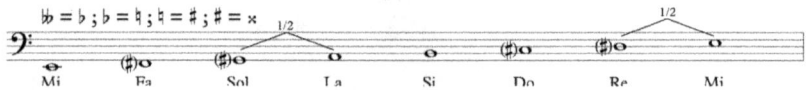

E-flat trumpet

Clef substitution: mezzo-soprano

Accidentals: lower all ½ step before Si (in mezzo-soprano clef)

E trumpet

Clef substitution: mezzo-soprano

Accidentals: raise all ½ step before Fa, Do, Sol, Re, La and Mi (in mezzo-soprano clef)

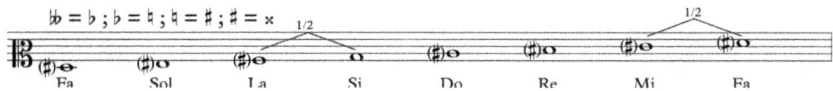

F trumpet

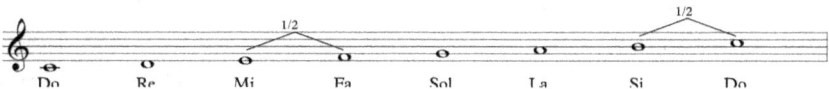

Clef substitution: baritone

Accidentals: raise all ½ step before Fa (in baritone clef)

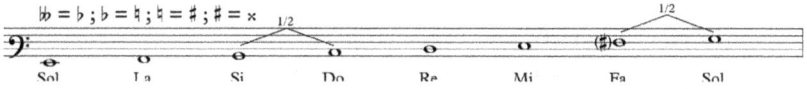

G-flat trumpet

Clef substitution: soprano

Accidentals: lower all ½ step before Si, Mi, La and Re (in soprano clef)

G trumpet

Clef substitution: soprano

Accidentals: raise all ½ step before Fa, Do and Sol (in soprano clef)

So, after all the clefs have been learned and all the rules about altering the appropriate accidentals have been learned, the problem of transposition is solved, right? To a large extent, yes. However, one of the main reasons transposition is difficult is that, as occurs similarly when sight-reading (which is dealt with elsewhere), our anxiety level goes up and we become product-oriented (not necessarily in that order). Our conscious mind plays dirty tricks. Not only do we suddenly feel disoriented by not knowing what we are about to play, but now we are also going to call all the notes by different names (with the substitution of another clef). Our conscious mind suddenly "forgets" everything: breathing, rhythm, pulse, articulation, tone, grouping, phrasing, nuance, end of note, etc. It is vital to reassure ourselves that we still do "know" everything else about playing the trumpet. It is essential to stay in the present and deal with process.

Rules

Rules are necessary for life. Rules are boundaries and guidelines that help establish structure. By knowing the rules, boundaries are defined. In that sense, they create freedom by defining what is allowed.

In society, rules are usually known as laws, which are established by governments—local, state, national—and cover many aspects of our lives. There are rules for grammar, math, driving, parking, and playing sports. It's important for a child to have rules and equally important for the parents to show consistency in defining and applying them. Without rules, there would be chaos!

Music also has rules. They are in the form of tonality (keys, tuning), rhythm (meter), dynamics, articulation, and style. In my theory of process, these are incorporated in the three basic concepts: shape, articulation, and grouping.

I first became aware of these rules concerning style while I was studying with William Vacchiano. He didn't specify that they were "rules," as such, but how notes were to be played in context. Although at the time these rules seemed to apply specifically to orchestral playing, they really are about music. A musician will adapt them to all repertoire: etudes, orchestral, chamber, brass quintets, and solo.

Shape

Quarter notes are long. Sixteenth notes are long. Unless specifically marked otherwise, eighth notes are always short (NB: eighths and sixteenths are identical).

The shape of a note is determined by its end, especially staccato (*detaché*) notes of short metric duration (for example, eighths and sixteenths). This was clarified in the section where tonguing was discussed.

Articulation

Articulation is how notes are connected, that is, by sound or silence. In groups of four notes (i.e., eighth or sixteenth notes, two slurred, two staccato), the second of the slurred notes is short (same shape as succeeding notes). Obviously, the first of the two slurred notes is <u>long</u>, so that the rhythm is not distorted (see "Grouping," below).

In groups of three notes, if the first and second are slurred, the second is short; if the second and third are slurred, the second is long, because it "belongs" to the next note.

If consecutive groups of two notes are slurred, with the pulse, the second is long (as in the "Ballerina Dance" in *Petrouchka*); if across the pulse, the second is short (Arban Characteristic Study #8).

Dotted rhythms are tricky and often inaccurately and carelessly played. Dotted eighths and sixteenths are differentiated by country (nationality). German (Austrian): sixteenth is heavier—almost like an eighth of a triplet. French: in a single-dotted eighth and sixteenth, the dotted eighth is long; if two or more in a group, the dotted eighth is short (as in the "March to the Scaffold" from Berlioz's *Symphony Fantastique*, for example). Italian: dotted eighth should be played like a double-dotted eighth and the sixteenth as a thirty-second. For example, Andre Kostelanetz rewrote the rhythms in Respighi's "The Pines of the Appian Way" from *The Pines of Rome* as double-dotted eighths and thirty-seconds to ensure they would be played stylistically accurately (note: although Mahler was Austrian, he often treats dotted eighths and sixteenths more like an Italian).

In music by Hungarian composers, one will often see written a *dotted eighth and sixteenth followed by a sixteenth and dotted eighth* (written) that is played as a *dotted eighth (long) and sixteenth as written, but sixteenth, dotted eighth played as a thirty-second and double-dotted eighth*. It is possible that this notation was meant to capture the rhythm that was played by Romani or in folk songs (e.g., "Intermezzo" from *Háry János* by Zoltán Kodály).

Then there is the dotted eighth-sixteenth-eighth as a triplet or compound meter (i.e., 3/8, 6/8, 12/8, etc.), which is often rendered inaccurately, such as in Beethoven's *Symphony No. 7*, Wagner's *Ride of the Valkyries*, etc. Thinking the word *Am-ster-dam* will render the rhythm correctly. The sixteenth (*"ster"*) is the critical note; if it is too early, it will change the rhythm to dotted sixteenth, thirty-second, eighth as a duple pattern. If it's too late, it will sound like a double-dotted eighth, thirty-second, eighth (or double-dotted quarter, sixteenth, quarter, as in the *Scherzo* of Bruckner's *Symphony No. 7*).

In any phrase or group of notes, the most important note is the one of shortest duration. It is vital that it has the same resonance and "weight" as the surrounding notes of longer value so that it doesn't get lost and go unheard.

Grouping

It is also critical that any note after the note on the pulse belongs to the next pulse. They are all anacruses. It is not only the pickup—the first note before the first bar line of a piece—that is the anacrusis.

Bar lines are for convenience of organizing notation visually into different meters, such as 2/4 (2/8), 3/4 (3/8), 4/4 (8/8), 5/4 (5/8), 6/4 (6/8), etc. They also determine where the emphasis or pulse will occur. Some composers (Olivier Messiaen comes to mind) compose without bar lines, and add bar lines and meter afterward.

Sometimes, composers beam notes across the pulse and/or even the bar lines. Although this is probably intended to produce the appropriate inflection and forward motion, it also will likely have the tendency to confuse the performer.

When notes are grouped according to the bar lines, beams, or articulation markings, the result will be what I call *pogo stick* (or vertical) phrasing; the phrasing will be static. There will be no forward motion or flow to the phrase.

I prefer to think in terms of anacrusis rather than arsis/thesis. So, it is critical, as stated above, that every note after the one on the pulse belongs to the next pulse. As I said at the end of the "Articulation" section, in any group of notes or phrase the most important note is the one of shortest duration. It is therefore necessary to emphasize these notes so that they sound equal. Up close, it might sound exaggerated, but further away, depending on the room acoustics, those little notes will have the appropriate balance in the phrase. (If the composers didn't think those shorter notes were important, they wouldn't have bothered writing them.) The shorter notes will enhance the notes of longer duration.

The acoustics/resonance of the performance space will also have an effect on what is required. Being aware of how the notes are grouped will allow inflection and nuance to enhance music-making. So again, thinking of the end of the note incorporates how the notes are shaped, connected, and grouped.

Phrasing

The trumpet player's vocabulary is not set. There is only a nuance of difference between "articulation" and "phrasing," and also "interpretation." Articulation and especially grouping are integral parts of phrasing. Students must learn the different types of phrasing they'll need in the art of interpretation. Punctuation allows the player to conceive of and play a sequence of notes in such a way that gives meaning to it, as the sentence gives meaning to the words that produce it.

My goal is not to indulge in conceptual distinctions. I simply want to stress the need for a concept: an understanding of the interdependence of the parts and the whole in music. Interdependence: it goes both ways—the words are the building blocks that make it possible to construct the sentence. The sentence gives new meaning to the words.

The following diagram of a wall reminds us that the whole is made up of parts. But this diagram gives too static a view and cannot suggest the complex and subtle relationships between the parts and the whole.

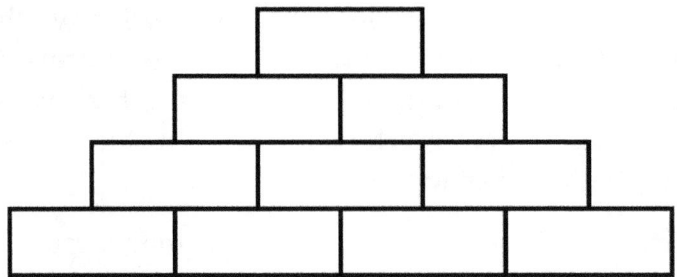

- This diagram symbolizes some of the ideas we shall go into here: the bottom row represents the bar lines defining the measures/bars (4 blocks), but also reflects and organizes the pulse, which is determined by meter and tempo.
- The second row represents the rhythmical grouping of long and short notes, or how the notes are beamed within each pulse, and how these groupings coincide or overlap with the defined bars or with the defined beats (we'll come back to pulse below).
- The third row corresponds to the actual grouping of the notes, contrary to how the notes are beamed, which, in most cases, will depend on subdivisions of the pulse.
- The top row represents articulation (staccato, slurred, legato).

In other words, this diagram of a wall illustrates how the bricks must overlap to give it maximum strength. This is also how a phrase should be conceived. The phrase overlaps the bar lines, the grouping of the notes overlaps the beamings, and the articulation overlaps the groupings.

For example, if, in building a wall, all the blocks were aligned on top of each other (instead of overlapping), the wall would be weak and easily toppled. Similarly, if the phrases were made to coincide with the bar lines and the grouping of the notes were confined within the beamings, and the articulation were played literally, then the phrase would be weak and have no forward motion. This latter type of phrasing is what I call *pogo stick phrasing*. You use a lot of energy, but you don't go anywhere.

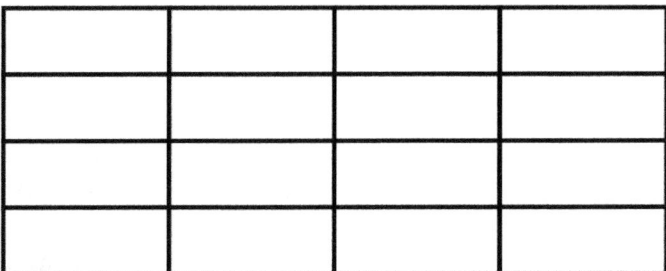

Back to the problem of vocabulary, let us go into some more distinctions. In music, the word "phrase" can either be a noun or a verb. If it's a noun, it's a sequence of notes that goes over the boundaries of one bar. It usually takes something like two to four bars. If the phrase is a verb, it then refers to taking a breath—or at least punctuating not by accents but by commas, question marks, exclamation marks, or periods. A "verb" also has to do with nuance and inflection.

In writing, the letters of the alphabet are arranged into words, the words are then organized into sentences, and then sentences into paragraphs, paragraphs into chapters, etc. In music, only the first seven letters of the alphabet are used (A, B, C, D, E, F, G), and with the addition of the sharps and flats, the number of notes reaches 12 different basic pitches. These can be arranged into melodies and organized into an almost infinite number of combinations and rhythmic patterns (words). These are organized into phrases (sentences), then are put together into different forms—introduction, exposition, development, recapitulation, coda, etc., which correspond, in writing, to paragraphs and chapters, etc.

Punctuation is an aspect of phrasing. Punctuation must be used in conjunction with pulse. In writing, we do not simply apply rules of punctuation as we first discovered at school. Back then, we then thought all this was just a matter of applying set rules. It is only later on that the reader of novels or other sorts of literature discovers that punctuation has something to do with the rhythm inherent in the sequence of written words. One experiences this especially acutely when reading a text aloud. In the case of a musical score, why then would we play the notes like a dry list of names in a phone book or of words in a dictionary? Music is both poetry and prose, which require pulse, punctuation, nuance, and inflection.

I teach my students to always keep an internal pulse going by tapping their foot at a steady tempo, becoming their own metronome. Even outside the ballroom, music is still dancing. A rhythmic pattern emerges, and as soon as we relate it to the pulse, music starts to live and breathe. Pierre Boulez once spoke about a whole generation of keyboard players who had discovered Bach but interpreted it in a way of playing that he aptly called the "sewing machine style."

Phrasing brings life to music and music to life. But what is *phrasing*? Phrasing is grouping and accentuating notes. It is adding inflections in the right spots. It is breathing. Unfortunately, "classical" training can often repress these qualities in young players. Classical music must be played *straight*, although those same young players often show a talent for phrasing when they play jazz or other, less *rigid*, forms of music.

I first heard the term *inflection* from William Vacchiano. Conductors don't seem to use the word very often, but most of them try to convey the use of inflection through the gestures they use in conducting—they indicate in coded form or personal ways what it means.

I like to use the word *inflection* extensively, and I explain it partly in terms of what I call the shape of the notes. This is, again, a way of entering a paradox, because by dealing with shapes of notes we deal with phrasing. But phrasing is how we group the notes we have shaped. In fact, it is more than grouping; it also has to do with articulation, nuance, timbre, and inflection. Shaping the notes differentiates one note from another while attending to the way they are connected.

Longer note values, such as whole notes, half notes, and quarter notes, are easier to shape, mainly because they are of longer duration—we have more time to deal with the shaping, as well as their connection.

When notes are of shorter duration, such as eighths, sixteenths, thirty-seconds, or even grace notes, it is potentially more difficult to define their shapes (differentiation), and therefore their connections.

The shapes of detached (staccato) notes must be determined by their ends, not their beginnings. This can only be accomplished by the tongue determining the end of the note (compared with tonguing).

As discussed in the section on articulation, consecutive staccato and legato notes are connected by silence.

Anyone listening or just hearing—without even trying to analyze—realizes how much the shape of the notes that build a musical phrase can vary. There are limitations to the variety achieved in this way, but one is usually surprised at what an immense difference the shapes of the notes alone can make. Low or high notes, slow or fast notes, big or small intervals, will all sound different if we change the shape of the notes. The figure below suggests three ways of ending the note:

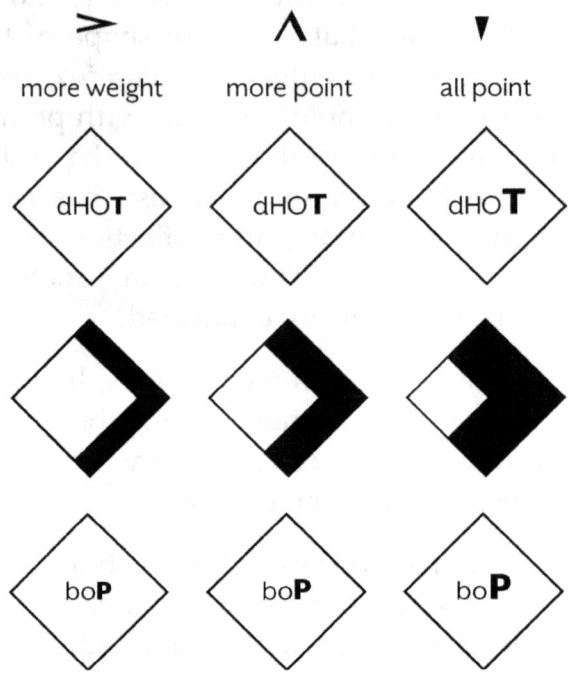

As mentioned, legato notes are also connected by silence, but the ratio between the sound and the silence is greater. In consecutive staccato notes, the proportion of the length of the note and the silence that connects it to the next note is equal to, or could be longer than, the duration of the note, which would of course depend on the tempo. Legato notes, on the other hand, are always much longer than the silence that connects them.

Once we are aware of shaping individual notes, the next step is to connect them appropriately when they are in groups.

One cannot live creatively without any rules. In fact, rules can and will permit even more freedom. So, here is my number one rule: keep with the pulse; any notes that come after the note on the pulse are pickups (anacruses) to the next pulse. If the phrase is comprised of only notes on the pulse, the next larger framework (the measures) will determine the grouping. In 4/4, 2 goes to 3; 4 goes to l; if 3/4 is the pattern, 2 goes to 3; 3 goes to 1, etc.

In ascending sequences, the higher notes often take on more importance because of their acoustical prominence. In other cases, the longer notes may seem more important (simply because they use more time and space). One must be careful, though, to avoid the obvious, because there may be other notes in the phrase that should receive more attention. In fact, here I would like to state a second rule that is rarely recognized by students and even by professionals.

Rule number two: in any group of notes, the most important is the shortest one. The logic supporting this (particularly if a valve change is involved) is that if the length of the vibrating air column changes, then the player must ensure that the air in the tubing (opened by the depressing of a valve) is set into vibration. But even more important, it is necessary to ensure the note of shorter duration is heard equally with the longer notes. The short notes must be in tune with and have the same resonance, color, and depth as the longer notes. Generally, shorter notes will have more intensity because of the articulation or rhythm, but they often have more intensity because of too much velocity, a remnant of early experience (anxiety or panic over playing "blacker" notes [i.e., more beams]). It will be necessary to make sure the tone itself is not too intense on the short notes. But, if the composer didn't consider the little notes important, they would not be there. This sometimes amounts to recognizing the importance of grace notes. Although these notes may at first seem like unnecessary decorations, in fact they determine the character of the sequence played.

Question: Why do you insist your students develop an understanding of the harmonic structure of a piece?

I do it to help them understand the direction in a line of notes. As in the structure of a sentence, in which the words lead to a meaning, the sequence of notes leads someplace, follows a path. The player, even the pure instrumentalist who does not plan to compose or arrange, should know enough about the chords involved to improve his phrasing and intonation. They should understand what they are invited to say in playing a certain score.

Ideally, the student should, eventually, understand the structure of the piece they play. Starting first with small sequences, they gradually come to discover the meaning of longer sequences and sequences of sequences (the piece). A student's phrasing is reflective of their overall development and understanding. To this end, we have dozens of exercises in study books, such as the *Complete Conservatory Method for Cornet* by J. B. Arban; *Practical Studies* by Edwin Franko Goldman; *Top Tones for the Trumpeter* by Walter M. Smith; and *Trente-Six Études Transcendantes* by Théo Charlier, probably the best etudes of all. Learning different types of phrasing through these study books is a prerequisite to the actual job of being an interpreter.

Among the recurring difficulties of playing any instrument is the necessity to consciously or, more often unconsciously, control many levels at the same time. Reading problems lead to forgetting about proper breathing (and conversely, improper breathing can lead to reading problems). An interest in phrasing can lead to the neglect of proper timing. Coloring a group of notes differently may interfere with articulation, effective breathing, etc. Very often, students fall victim to oversimplification, and I have to refresh their approach by showing and explaining how much more interesting music can be than just playing notes as they are written on the page.

Here are a few of the reminders I often give students:

- You can shape the notes differently without changing their length.
- Think of where these notes go harmonically, but don't forget to also keep in mind the shape and the resonance of the notes.

Every now and then, whether we are preoccupied with phrasing or articulation, we have to return to basics (i.e., intonation):

- Pull the third slide for the low F-sharp and G, otherwise all the other notes will tend to go up; start playing slowly at the right place.
- You can avoid cracking these low notes if you focus on intonation—use the slides, not your lips, to make corrections.
- Don't forget your foot—it is hard to play in the right place if you don't know where that is.
- You don't fail to take in enough air because the abdomen is too tight, but because you were too worried about other things.
- When the intervals are wider, it takes more glue to slur (connect them with sound).

One more comment on the velocity of air flow: it is relevant in many sections of the trumpet player's work, but is of special importance in slow lyrical pieces in which we want to emphasize phrasing even more. Slurring (connecting notes with sound) wide intervals can be one of the more problematic areas for trumpet players, even though flexibility drills abound and rival long tones for the number of hours logged in practice. Increasing velocity is an integral part of the slurring process. However, players tend to wait until the slur is supposed to occur before increasing the velocity. I propose that players think of increasing the energy in the sound, either by making an ever-so-slight crescendo or by increasing the intensity before leaving the note to be connected by a slur to the following note, whether going up or down. Also, instead of trying to make a very clean slur—that is, not nicking any notes in between the two notes—try to get all the notes, as if making a *glissando*. First of all, the slur will sound much smoother, and even if it doesn't, there are times when a "shlurppy" slur is more desirable; it sometimes is referred to as a Viennese slur.

Warming Up

"What is the purpose of warming up?" When I have asked this of students, usually their answer is along the lines of getting the lips to vibrate, getting the embouchure loosened up, getting the fingers moving, getting the tongue working, etc. Rarely, if ever, does anyone say, "To get the breathing apparatus operating in the way necessary to play the instrument in the most efficient, relaxed manner possible."

Basically, the purpose of warming up is to set up the system so that we can play whatever is necessary throughout the day: producing our basic sound (tone) at all dynamic levels, through all articulations (slurring, tonguing—single, double, triple, etc.), fast or slow. What we play isn't as important as what we are thinking about. Whatever we play should serve as a template to indicate whether the system is working at maximum efficiency. Playing "exercises" will not make the system work, but it can contribute to doing more harm than good. I prefer to think of warming up as "checking the templates."

Inhaling is the most critical, essential part of warming up, since air is the raw material from which we produce sound. We are always breathing, but this will adjust according to our activity. It's involuntary; that is, it is natural. If we are sitting, standing, or sleeping, we are breathing according to our bodily needs. If we do something strenuous, such as running, swimming, riding a bicycle, etc., our breathing will increase in volume and rapidity — all without thinking, except while swimming, when the inhale must be coordinated with when our mouth is out of the water. Part of the problem of breathing with regard to playing the trumpet is that trumpet playing is a strenuous activity, but is usually done when sitting or standing (unless one is in a marching band). That creates a paradox. So, advising someone to breathe naturally doesn't work, because there is nothing natural about playing the trumpet. Often the advice is to "only take in the amount of air needed." The implication is: for the length of phrase to be played. What is omitted in that advice is that it's necessary to make the air column in the instrument (depending on the pitch of the instrument: B-flat, C, D, piccolo, etc.) vibrate at the appropriate frequency, volume, etc., for whatever length, volume, or register is required.

Additionally, it is necessary to satisfy our physical needs (the lungs still have to supply the oxygen necessary for the body to function and to exchange CO_2 in the process). It's also necessary to make sure our brain gets enough oxygen. Very often, a player will play a passage (in an etude or solo piece) until their air supply is exhausted and they make a "mistake," which only then justifies taking a breath. By this point, the player has run out of air to make a good sound on the trumpet and, just as importantly, the brain is oxygen-starved, which causes the player to miss the note. It is necessary to know when to take a breath. One must be able to phrase without breathing and breathe without phrasing.

Many people have a definite, set warm-up routine, which must be strictly followed to the point of compulsion. I have known players (professionals as well as students) who have had such extensive, demanding warm-ups that, by the time they were "warmed up," they were too tired to play a rehearsal or a concert.

For years, I used the same routine (the Gustat warm-up—see appendix) and was convinced that unless I got through the whole thing, I would not be able to function at my best. Warming up is as much mental as it is physical ... maybe more.

When playing in an orchestra rehearsal, those for whom a definite warm-up routine is a requirement may be in trouble if the conductor decides to rehearse the strings for a half hour, or if in a concert there are one or two tacet movements, after which the player is no longer warmed up but must play the next entrance as if they were.

For years, I dreaded the first notes of the day. I sometimes would pretend my first notes were the second notes. The solution came when I used the first note as an indicator of whether I had inhaled to the maximum. Once the first note is a "usable" note, for all practical purposes, the warm-up is successful.

Practicing

What is the purpose of practicing? It means working. It means being involved. Playing the trumpet (or any instrument) is not a spectator sport—it is participatory and requires concentration. One of the goals of practicing is to strive for maximum efficiency: to achieve maximum results with minimum effort.

Students are told to practice—by teachers, parents, and sometimes even by conductors. When I was a student at Juilliard, Jean Morel (conductor of the Juilliard Orchestra) once said "You must practice. It does no good to pray—God has no time for musicians."

When I began playing the trumpet, I practiced a lot—not necessarily with the idea that I would improve, but because it was fun! Sometimes my parents would beg me to stop. I quickly discovered that practicing would get me out of the household chores I didn't want to do. Later, when I was at Juilliard, practicing served as an escape mechanism: it took my mind off of being hungry, lonely, unhappy, insecure, or whatever. I could rationalize procrastinating the work for my classes by practicing for five, six, or even eight hours a day. So, practicing served many purposes for me. Improvement was one of the fortunate fringe benefits.

What to practice is not as important as how to practice. The reason for practicing is to become a better musician. The process of using these three basic concepts will help to achieve that goal. These concepts apply to all music. Whether practicing simple scales and arpeggios or etudes, solos, and orchestral pieces, it is necessary to be aware of how the notes are shaped, how they are connected, and how they are grouped.

Using the concepts will establish the content, because without establishing content, there can be no differentiation in the context. The content is tone and intonation, rhythm, dynamics, articulation, phrasing, style. The context is whatever music is being played. The whole is greater than the sum of its parts.

Thinking of the beginning of the note is product orientation. Thinking of the end of the note is process orientation.

"Practice makes perfect!"

What does that mean? What is perfect? Playing all the right notes? At the right time with the correct rhythm? In tune? What about articulation? What about phrasing, dynamics, timbre, nuance, inflection???

Perfection is a tall order. Perfection is the ultimate in product orientation. When I was about 18 years old, I discovered that perfection (at least for me) was not on my horizon. The ultimate goal is to make beautiful music, which is a process.

"You must practice every day."

"If you miss one day of practice, you can tell; if you miss two days, your parents can tell; if you miss three days, everyone can tell."

"You should practice one hour a day."

"You should practice two hours a day."

"You should practice four hours—six hours—eight hours—ten hours!"

When asked if he took his trumpet with him on holiday, a famous trumpet player replied, "Oh yes, I keep my trumpet right by my bed. Every morning, when I wake up, I pick it up and play 'toot-toot-toot,' if it feels good, I figure—why practice? If I pick it up and play 'toot-toot-toot,' and it feels terrible, I figure—why bother?"

I once had a student who couldn't play anything that I asked him to play during a lesson. When I scolded him, saying, "You really must practice more," he replied, on the verge of tears, "But I practiced an hour and a half every day!" At the next lesson he sounded terrific. I said "Wow, you must have really practiced more!" He responded, "Gosh, I've had so much schoolwork, I haven't touched the trumpet since the last lesson."

Many trumpet players are afraid to take time off, partially because they feel guilty for missing even a day or two. The concern is that not practicing will result in a loss of strength and then it will be necessary to get back in shape. Almost everyone who has taken a few days off will agree that, when they do return, everything is better: breathing, tone, tonguing, flexibility, etc. The concern is that those improvements won't last for more than a few minutes.

In my experience, it is not the strength that has diminished, but the relaxation of the muscles (and the brain) that has increased because the tension that can build up when playing every day has dissipated. It is generally agreed that the true strength of a muscle is the degree to which it can relax. Often, tension (tightness) is misinterpreted as strength. The problem with that interpretation is that instead of capitalizing on the newly acquired relaxed state, players tend to return to their inefficient ways of playing. Sometimes, practicing can reinforce negative habits.

After I have taken time off—sometimes a week or more—rather than trying to get back into shape, I pretend I haven't taken any time off. When I focus on music rather than mechanics and take advantage of the relaxed state, I can sustain the benefits of the time off. I have often found that after taking time off, I could play passages that I'd been struggling with before, on a daily basis, both better and with less effort.

Many people advise musicians to always think of playing for an audience. For me that is not practicing; that is performing, which often leads back to focusing on the product—perfection—rather than the process. But then, when actually performing, we tend to start thinking about what we're doing (practicing).

I think one should play for oneself. It places too big a burden on a musician to play for your parents, for your colleagues, for the conductor, for the audience, or for God. If making music is the top priority, the musician will be able to focus on the ingredients within the three concepts: shape, connection, grouping. The whole of those three is greater than the sum of its parts.

Musicians must have the courage to not always sound "good." By using their imagination to play with different dynamics, timbre, inflection, and nuance while practicing, one can explore a variety of interpretations to determine which ones might work in performance.

For example, the lyrical solo in *Don Juan* (Richard Strauss) is really meant to enhance what the violins are playing. It must blend with, but also reinforce, their melody. Likewise, the lyrical solo in the first movement of Mahler's *Fifth Symphony* is really meant to enhance the viola solo. So, it's not just a matter of the dynamic but also of the timbre, intonation, and rhythm. These excerpts illustrate one of the main goals for practicing—understanding the context and content when developing technique for scales, arpeggios, etudes, solos, or orchestral music. In other words, music must take precedence in whatever we play.

As stated before, there is no product in music. Whatever, or however, one plays, whether fantastic or horrible, it is gone as soon as you have played it. Even if it is recorded, there is no product—it is a reproduction.

Music is a process! It is like writing or reading a story. It is painting a picture. It is taking a trip, or rather traveling—a journey. It is cooking a meal (whether gourmet or not). It is sewing or weaving. It is building a piece of furniture or a house. It is gardening. But it is in the world of sound. There is nothing concrete. But still it can be pleasurable, satisfying, gratifying, and rewarding. It is playing! But it is also work. Unfortunately, sometimes it can also be very frustrating. Practice is work. But it is also play. For a young child, play is work. For a musician, this is a paradox. We play an instrument—but we have to work at it. Practice is learning—and learning requires practice.

So, how do we practice? How do we learn?

Learning is also a process. There are three primary modes for learning: visual, aural, and kinesthetic. For each person, one of these modes is dominant or primary (e.g., one whose dominant mode is visual would say, " I see what you mean"; one whose dominant mode is aural would say, "I hear what you're saying"; one whose dominant mode is kinesthetic might say, "That feels right"). There is one more learning mode: olfactory. Information acquired through this mode goes directly to the cerebral cortex. Most people have experienced a particular odor that triggers a panorama of memories, complete with emotional responses. If only we could learn to play the trumpet through the olfactory mode! (Note: For anyone wishing to pursue more detailed information concerning learning modes, there are books dealing with that subject.)

There are many things that can be learned only through the kinesthetic mode: riding a bicycle, driving a car, skating, etc. One cannot learn to do these things visually or aurally. Neither looking at nor listening to a bicycle, a car, or a pair of skates will make you proficient at these skills—they can only be developed through muscle memory. Similarly, rhythm (or pulse, or beat) must be learned kinesthetically. You rarely hear someone speak in terms of *hearing* or *seeing* the beat, only *feeling* the beat. In that sense, "feeling the beat" is not just an expression!

Rhythm is not just playing specific patterns in a steady tempo. Rhythm is also what coordinates our breathing, lips, fingers, tongue, eyes, and ears. And yet, very often, students are advised, "Don't 'beat' your foot." I would concur with this advice pertaining to performance. But, when practicing, if it is not done, how will one learn to internalize the pulse (or beat)?

Usually, the use of a metronome is suggested. If it were possible to learn rhythm through the visual or aural mode, this would work. Unfortunately, if one is dependent on this external source for pulse, then when it's not there, neither will the pulse be. So, unless one is overdubbing in a recording studio and playing with a click track, the metronome stays at home also.

I recommend against playing with a metronome. However, if one feels insecure about one's rhythm or ability to maintain a steady tempo, there is a way to practice using a metronome. For example, one could turn on the metronome but, instead of playing with it, either clap or tap the foot with it, so that it can't be heard. If the metronome can be heard, the player is not keeping a steady pulse. But, by physically (kinesthetically) experiencing the beat, one will learn to recognize when there is any deviation. In fact, the player becomes their own metronome.

At this point, a comment about metronome markings is appropriate. Most everyone agrees that creativity is an unconscious (right brain) function. This, obviously, includes composing. Except for those composers who compose film soundtracks (for soundtracks, the music must fit into a prescribed time period) and who use metric modulation as a compositional technique, no composer writes with a metronome marking (exact tempo) in mind. The tempo indication is added after the fact. It has been my experience that most metronome markings are too fast, whether for etudes, solos, chamber music, or orchestral works. In some cases, it might be too slow. A much more valid indication for tempo is what the composer has written (such as allegro, andante, presto, largamente, etc.), which also indicates a feeling or character, as well as an approximate tempo.

The most important reason for becoming your own metronome (i.e., beating your foot, and making yourself keep up with your foot) is that you will stay in the present. Staying in the present is the most vital part of the process. The present is the connection between the past (what you just played) and the future (what you are about to play). It is impossible to be in two places at one time. If you worry about what you just played (or missed) or what lies ahead (you might miss), your chances of missing what you are supposed to be playing right now increase greatly. Staying in the present also eliminates anxiety. There is no anxiety in the present. Anxiety exists in the past (worrying about what you just played) or in the future (worrying about what you are about to play), neither of which you can do anything about until the next time you play it in the present. Staying in the present will also prevent you from activating the internal judges (e.g., "That was great" and "That was terrible"). The most harmful judge is the benevolent one, the voice that says, "That was great!" You are being set up for failure. A giant banana peel appears for you to step and slip on or, as if there were a virtual attachment between your wrist and your ankle, the degree to which you pat yourself on the back determines how far up the kick will come, to your shin, your knee, your stomach, or your mouth!

One can learn without understanding and understand without learning! What does this mean?

Some players can learn in practice what a teacher said, but they don't understand why a certain way of playing "worked." On the other hand, some students are perfectly capable of mentally understanding what a teacher wants them to do and why, but they are unable to put into practice what is suggested. Knowledge is when understanding and learning become one.

Thinking of the beginning of the note is product orientation. Thinking of the end of the note is process orientation.

Anxiety

There are two kinds of anxiety: chronic and acute.

Chronic anxiety is built into our systems. We carry it inside us—it is always there. It has accumulated since birth from our own experience, and is even passed on from our families. It is in our heads and stems from anything we perceive as a threat, or potential threat, including fear of disease, fear of hunger, and fear of rejection.

Acute anxiety stems from tangible threats in the external world. These threats can be anything: an aggressive animal, physical/emotional threats from another human, a potential car accident, or, most relevant to the topic at hand, playing an audition or performing in an important concert.

One indication of an elevated anxiety level is being very critical and judgmental of ourselves and others. We all have built-in judges. Often these take the form of voices in our heads, telling us what we have done or are doing wrong. The emotional response to acute anxiety is always the same, though: fight or flight.

Performance anxiety manifests in many forms and can be elevated by different triggers. It is sometimes referred to as stage fright, jitters, performance nerves, or panic. Each of these symptoms is an example of the psychological (emotional) manifestation of anxiety. The physical symptoms can include (but are certainly not limited to): sweaty palms, dry mouth (ropey saliva), tension, tremors (shakes), nausea (vomiting), and even diarrhea. But the first thing that is affected is the breathing apparatus. The term "a knot in the stomach" is pretty accurate. Anxiety will cause the involuntary muscles of the breathing apparatus to tighten, severely limiting our ability to inhale.

Concentrating on breathing (inhaling) helps keep the conscious mind occupied and the whole physical system well supplied with oxygen, which will contribute to the body's innate ability to eliminate muscular tension. Strictly speaking, there is no anxiety in the present. There is anxiety about the past—when one worries about what was just played (evaluating or judging), and there is anxiety about the future—when one worries about what is about to be played. There is also a combination of the two: worrying about what is coming, as well as what you have experienced difficulty with in the past.

One cannot stay in the present by concentrating on the present.

One of the ways to stay in the present is to tap your foot (toe, not heel). Using one's foot is not only for counting, it is also for coordinating all the small muscle movements necessary for playing, in the eyes, ears, mouth (embouchure), tongue, and fingers (on both hands to operate valves and slides). Keeping time with your foot will also keep you in the present. If you play a note exactly as the foot touches the floor, it will not be necessary to think about each of the individual physical movements required to attack (commence) the tone.

It is also necessary to use the appropriate foot. The brain has two hemispheres: for right-handed people, the left hemisphere controls the conscious mind, and the right hemisphere controls the unconscious mind. By using the left foot, one may tap into the unconscious mind, where knowledge is stored. The sound will be more beautiful with less effort, less *thinking*. Essentially, the left foot stimulates the process (making music) and the right stimulates the product (analyzing, judging, etc.). If a person is right-handed, they will achieve noticeably more musical success by tapping their left foot. Left-handed people are generally the opposite and will benefit from tapping their right foot.

Using one's imagination with the musical aspects of one's playing (tone, dynamics, nuances, phrasing, etc.), rather than simply striving for accuracy, will keep the conscious mind occupied with things other than worrying. When the conscious mind is otherwise occupied, the unconscious mind will be able to guide you to do what you have trained yourself to do, uninhibited by anxiety. Allowing the unconscious mind to guide the musician while the conscious mind is occupied represents inductive—rather than deductive—thinking and reduces analysis and judgment of one's action while it is occurring, therefore helping to reduce—rather than increase—the anxiety level. The use of imagination that must be incorporated into this type of concentration must be learned during practice.

Self-hypnosis is another way of reducing anxiety. There is nothing mysterious, exotic, or even dangerous about hypnosis. Put simply, hypnosis is an altered state of consciousness that most people experience sometimes or even regularly—even if they are not aware of it. For example, have you ever walked or driven to a friend's house to discuss the vacation you are planning to take together, and been so deeply engrossed in imagining how much fun you will have that you are suddenly at your friend's house, and you don't remember anything you saw on the way or even which route you took to their house? This is sometimes referred to as "being on automatic pilot." This is actually a hypnotic trance. When the conscious mind is completely occupied or absorbed, the unconscious mind will still be able to function and to do what it has "learned" to do. This is also true for playing the trumpet. If, while practicing, one actively uses the conscious mind to be imaginative and curious about timbre, nuance, shaping, articulation, and phrasing, the unconscious mind will do the actual playing. This active participation will help reduce anxiety. This is a cursory example of self-hypnosis. Anyone wishing to pursue hypnosis further must find someone who is highly trained and qualified in hypnosis.

A few years ago, some beta blocker experiments were done on musicians. The primary application for beta blockers is treating people who suffer from hypertension, high blood pressure, irregular heartbeat, and other cardiovascular conditions. Because beta blockers selectively block adrenaline receptors, they may also be used to limit anxiety. Beta blockers don't reduce anxiety the way tranquilizers do, but they can reduce the jolt that adrenaline normally produces and thus reduce the symptoms usually associated with adrenaline surges. For some players, taking beta blockers allows them to perform as if under optimum conditions, even in the most stressful conditions. Beta blockers will *not* enable a person to do anything they cannot already do. Beta blockers do not make the player feel generally calmer (again, beta blockers are not tranquilizers), but if the player misses a note or has some other malfunction, the usual emotional jolt that normally results from the rush of adrenaline will not occur, and the player can continue to function optimally. It is important to note that beta blockers can have adverse effects on those who suffer from asthma or extremely low blood pressure, and should be used only under a doctor's supervision.

Another instantaneous way to reduce anxiety is to pinch the "webbing" (fleshy part) between the thumb and forefinger of one hand using the thumb and forefinger of the other hand. The level of pain this produces is an indicator of one's anxiety level. When the pain subsides, repeat the process, increasing the pressure each time, until there is no more pain. This should be done on each hand. Usually, one side will hurt more than the other, but not necessarily. You will immediately notice the decrease in anxiety.

Auditions

An audition is the most unrealistic performance any musician will ever face. Why is it unrealistic? About 60 years ago, someone came up with the idea of Music Minus One recordings. For example, the recording features a brass quintet minus the first trumpet part, so one could play along with the recordings at home to get the "experience" of playing with an ensemble. An orchestral audition is Music Minus One-Hundred. Often it is one of the shortest performances anyone will do—10 to 30 minutes—and it has the potential to have the most profound impact on one's professional career.

An audition is also part of the process of applying to conservatories for admission to study and prepare for a position in a symphony orchestra. For this type of audition, the musician usually will play a couple of etudes, one or two solo pieces, and three or four orchestral excerpts. When auditioning for an orchestra, the etudes usually are omitted, although in some recent orchestra auditions, etudes have been requested. In the United States, the repertoire for preliminary through semifinal and final rounds of auditions is derived primarily from significant orchestral passages. In the final round, the musician will usually be asked to play a solo work; occasionally, the musician will also be asked to play chamber music with the section or, in some cases, with the full orchestra. In many European orchestras, the emphasis is on solo rather than orchestral literature.

In the "good old days," that is, prior to 50 years ago, when an orchestra had an opening, the conductor might call a teacher of whatever instrumental position was open and ask if he (in those days most of the teachers were men, and most of the prospective orchestral musicians were men) had any students who were "ready." If the teacher had someone to recommend, that was that. No further audition! In the mid-1960s, orchestra members got more involved in the workings of their orchestras, including the audition process. This resulted in the formation of audition committees that had some input on auditions. In most cases, the committees would hear preliminary rounds of auditions and vote on which candidates should be advanced (in the late 1970s, orchestras started allowing taped recordings to be used for preliminary rounds). Today, the conductor (music director) hears only the final round and has the final say as to who will be hired. Even though a committee still votes on a candidate, very often this is only "advisory."

Regardless of the format, auditioning can be one of the most stressful, anxiety-raising, frustrating, and (depending on the outcome) either depressing or exhilarating experiences a musician will ever have.

There are some musicians who can play a "great" audition (no anxiety, note-perfect playing), but have little or no experience, or even awareness, of performing in an ensemble. This often results in the "winner" not keeping the job. On the other hand, there are players who perform at a very high artistic level, but in an audition experience almost debilitating anxiety. Probably the musicians who are most prepared to audition are those just out of the conservatories, because they have been studying and practicing orchestral repertoire, though in most cases, they have not had much actual "performance experience." One would think, then, that years of professional experience would give musicians the upper hand at an audition. That is not necessarily the case. It used to be said that the conductor "wants someone 20 years old with 25 years of experience." Nowadays, the conductor very often wants someone 20 years old with no experience, so they can mold the musician—which rarely, if ever, works. It seems to be the consensus that older players are not flexible, which is not the case at all. The older player with experience is able to be more flexible because of having played with many different conductors. Another negative trait attributed to the "experienced" player is that the longer one plays in a professional environment, the more difficult it is to play a naked audition. Psychologically, this person may regress to their first audition and feel insecure and uncomfortable being tested. While regression can be reversed or controlled, dealing with it adds to the complexities that auditions bring with them and complicates the ordeal.

That said, auditioning is currently a fact of life. If someone wants to pursue an orchestral career, they have to learn how to present themselves in the most positive manner when playing an audition.

So, how should that be done? First, it is assumed that when a musician decides to audition, they have achieved a fairly high level of proficiency on their instrument and an awareness of both music in general and the orchestral repertoire in particular. In a time frame of anywhere from about ten minutes to a half hour, the musician must be able to demonstrate their credentials: make a positive, personal, musical statement that encompasses sound, style, rhythm, dynamics, phrasing, and, of course, interpretation.

So how does one prepare for an audition? It has been said that if one is prepared, there will be no anxiety. The implication of this adage is that if you know and can play the repertoire, everything will be fine.

Although audition issues are similar for all players, the following comments pertain particularly to trumpet players.

When a candidate spends hours practicing the repertoire while striving to achieve a state of perfection (accuracy), it can, in some cases, result in antipathy (even hatred) or a phobia toward certain excerpts. In these hours of practice, the candidate may ignore (or take for granted) the basic requisites that have made them a fine player, such as their breathing, concept of tone, articulation, dynamics, phrasing, and nuance. They can become totally focused on the product at the expense of the process.

Unfortunately, there is no product when we play an instrument. If it comes out fantastic, it's gone; if it comes out less than fantastic, it is also gone.

Unfortunately, our minds also will dredge up feelings from the first time we played in public and recreate that emotional state. It's that emotional state that can cause things to go terribly awry at an audition.

Next are some criteria pertinent to auditioning.

Accuracy

Accuracy, of course, is important, and because of today's digital recordings, editing can produce flawless, note-perfect renditions. Rarely, if ever, are any mistakes heard on recordings.

This is probably one of the reasons accuracy has an excessive degree of importance today—it is almost an obsession.

What does accuracy mean? If the musician plays no wrong notes—but does not play with any nuance, inflection, timbre, or awareness of style, characteristics that would make their playing an artistic musical interpretation—they may, in fact, be "missing" all the notes.

Dynamics

The advice "avoid dynamic extremes" is sometimes given. The only reason someone would recommend this would be in pursuit of playing it safe, that is, not taking chances.

But what does this lead to? If a marking of *fff* is rendered *f*, or *ppp* is played *p*, then the committee/conductor will probably think either that this person has a very limited dynamic range, that this person is not paying attention to what the composer has written, or that the person is being overly cautious.

Although there is absolutely no consensus as to a precise decibel level for each dynamic, the candidate must show they are capable of playing at all dynamic levels, including at the extremes. Dynamics are also relative to the composer. A *ff* in a Beethoven symphony is not as loud as a *ff* in a Mahler symphony. It is necessary to establish the relative dynamic range according to composer and context. An integral part of dynamics is timbre, which is often overlooked or ignored. Timbre is one of those areas that is hard to verbalize. It can mean resonance (darkness), intensity (brilliance), or a combination of the two. It can be achieved with vibrato or changing the velocity (speed) of the air. There is also a quality of intensity that is determined by articulation or rhythm; for example, staccato (*detaché*) notes have more intensity than legato or slurred notes, and sixteenth notes have more intensity than quarter notes or half notes. The acoustics of the venue in which the audition is played also will affect the person auditioning. If an audition is played in an empty concert hall, the amount of reverberation can be distracting.

What is the Committee And/or Conductor Looking For?

If this question goes through your mind as you begin playing, your anxiety level will likely rise significantly. It is up to you, the musician, to show the committee/conductor what you can do, and it is up to the committee/conductor to decide whether what you can do is what they are looking for.

Showing What You Can Do

A candidate must play with a beautiful sound, a strong rhythmic sense, a wide variety of articulation, and a wide range of dynamics and timbre. Intelligent phrasing and an awareness of style, combined with all of the above, will display the candidate's personal musicianship and understanding of interpretation.

Audition for the Experience?

There are no two auditions alike, so the experience acquired will probably not be directly useful for future auditions.

For a simulation of the audition experience, try this: Stand at a bus stop. Step out into the street as the bus approaches. Stay in its path until it is about ten feet away. Jump back to the curb! This will give you a tremendous rush of adrenaline, similar to what you would experience at an audition. Try at your own risk; the author claims no responsibility or liability!

Anxiety and Auditions

That said, there are still going to be trumpet players who will want to audition "for the experience." Why? Probably because of their belief that only participation in the real thing will help in overcoming audition anxiety.

Anxiety (or, as it is known by its other names, stage fright, performance nerves, etc.) will manifest itself in auditions more so than in regular performances, such as rehearsals or concerts. An audition is the ultimate anxiety-raising situation with which we have to cope. Our credentials are being examined, tested, challenged, and ultimately judged. Our future is at stake. Our reputation is on the line. It is a kind of competition, a contest. We must prove ourselves in a highly competitive context where we are compared to other candidates.

In everyday practice, it is essential that the player develop the skills for countering the side effects of anxiety. It is too late to deal with the anxiety at an actual audition. The effects of anxiety must first be understood in general. Anxiety is a type of fear often described through expressions like "a knot in one's stomach." This is not just an expression. If anxiety is not dealt with and dissipated, it will be somatized. That is, the anxiety will be "pushed" into the muscles, making them tense. The muscles of the stomach and abdomen do indeed contract to form a knot. And anxiety can cause one to almost stop breathing, which will raise one's anxiety level. In addition to a negative effect on breathing, anxiety can cause the heart rate to increase dramatically, the blood pressure to rise, the palms to perspire, and the mouth to become dry or to secrete ropey saliva.

What to Do?

Most trumpet players tend not to inhale nearly enough on a regular basis. It is often overlooked (or not learned or acknowledged) that the body—and the brain—require oxygen to function efficiently, so it's even more important to inhale to the maximum potential. It has been said that taking in too much air will make one tight. In fact, it only makes one aware of how tight they already are. Therefore, it is necessary to get rid of (or minimize) tension. This can be achieved only by focusing on inhaling regularly. It's too late to suddenly think about this at an audition.

Air is the raw material from which sound is created. The function of the lips (embouchure) is to make the air in the instrument vibrate at the appropriate frequency to play the notes. If the player inhales insufficiently, the result will be too much velocity in expelling the air (playing). This will result in notes that do not speak, are missing, or have too much intensity (which will produce incorrect or inappropriate dynamics). When a note doesn't speak, the trumpet player will usually experience this as the lips not vibrating. Actually, the air is moving too fast for the lips to make the air in the trumpet vibrate at the appropriate speed to produce the appropriate note. Thus, when anxiety compounds the effect of neglected inhalation due to added tightness, one does not—indeed, cannot—play at the level required.

When practicing in general (not necessarily for an audition), it is important never to try to play anything exactly the same way twice (first, it's impossible, and second, why would anyone want to?). If a musician (trumpet player) spent time analyzing the music rather than their mechanics, much more knowledge would be gained and their performance skills would be enhanced. One may be obligated to play the same notes, the same rhythms (not necessarily the same tempi), but one should always try to do something different with nuance, inflection, phrasing, dynamics, and timbre, within the context of what the composer has written. Even when practicing scales and arpeggios, attention must be given to rhythm, intonation, articulation, inflection, and dynamics. If one learns to practice this way (using the imagination), there will be several fringe benefits: (1) practicing will become more enjoyable, (2) the conscious mind will be occupied with something other than being judgmental, thus the anxiety level will likely be lower, and (3) in this way, not only will consistency (accuracy) be achieved, but, when this approach is used when preparing for an audition, the performance will sound more creative, spontaneous, and fresh. Best of all, there will be many "choices" for the actual performance. This applies not only to etudes but also to solos and orchestral repertoire.

If this approach to practicing is pursued, it can be applied to repertoire for auditioning purposes and performing in general. The focus will be on making music, not just on "not missing" any notes.

After acquiring all the necessary skills (i.e., proficiency on the instrument, audition experience, handling anxiety, presenting musical credentials in the best possible manner), then what? There is always luck! I played auditions that I thought were terrific, but I didn't win the auditions. There were auditions when I thought I didn't stand a chance because of how terribly I had played, and I got the job! So, if someone says to you, "Good luck on the audition," by all means accept it!

Afterword:
The End of the Note

The original title for this book was *Zen and the Art of the Trumpet: A Conceptual Process from A–Z*. Although it is now called *Indirection,* it still is, like life itself, about process. It is also about relationships, about cumulative learning, and about emerging complexity.

Thinking about the "end of the note" is the ultimate use of indirection. How does one think about the end of the note? I have no idea. It is a concept; it is Zen. But I know it combines the three basic concepts: shaping, articulation (connecting), and grouping.

The New England Conservatory of Music is abbreviated NEC, although students have invented a number of alternate meanings like *Not Exactly College* or, when Laurence Lesser was president, *Not Enough Cellos*. One of my early students, though, said it meant *Note End Concept*. Thinking of the end of the note includes the beginning and the middle and the end—without thinking about each. The whole is greater than the sum of its parts. It provides a different way of thinking: inductive rather than deductive. It requires imagination. It requires curiosity. It does not require an answer. There is no answer. There is no product.

I do know that when I think about the ends of notes, it changes my playing in a positive way. When I tell a student to think of the end of the note, it changes their playing too, regardless of their native language. It is a concept; it is process; it is imagination. It doesn't feel like you are doing anything, but it works. It makes everything easier. But if you stop doing whatever it is, playing will again be more difficult.

The primary goal of becoming a musician is to make beautiful music, and thinking about the end of the note has been critical to that process for me and for my students. Since the prime element of music is sound, it is crucial to develop one's own unique sound. This is true of all instruments and for all styles of music. It is the identity for all musicians—their personality, their signature.

third intermission

My first Monette C trumpet, #005. Charlie Gorham got #001 and #002. I eventually acquired #003, which was Dave's first Eb trumpet; Adolph (Bud) Herseth, principal trumpet in the Chicago Symphony Orchestra for over 50 years, got #004. My #005 arrived in 1983, which convinced me to only play Monette piston trumpets for the rest of my professional life.

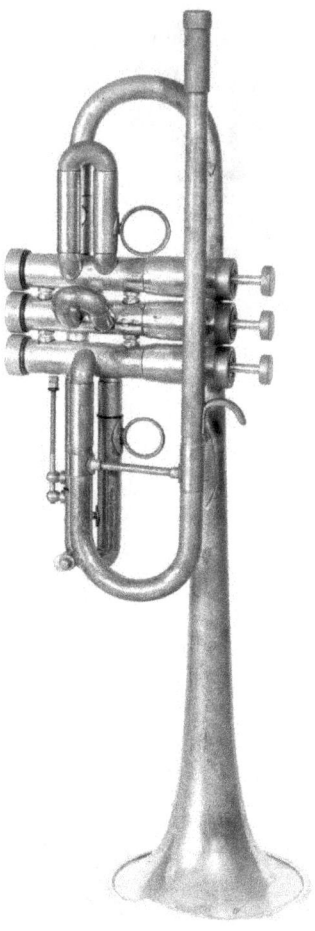

This trumpet, #061, inspired a model number: 61X, which became one of the most popular Monette trumpets for years.

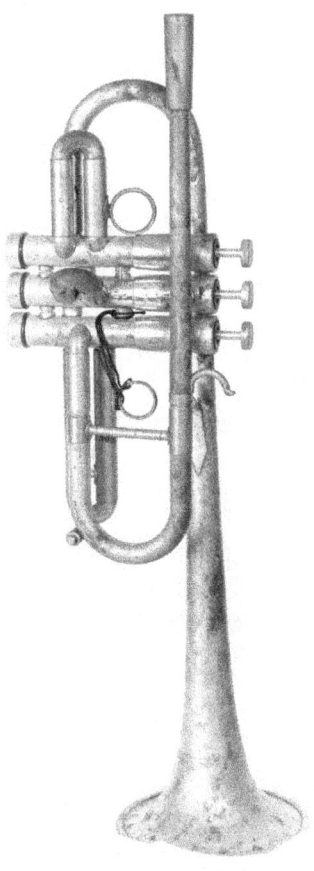

My 50th birthday STC2, #617, which was Dave Monette's first STC2 trumpet. It was given the number 617 for sentimental reasons. 617 was the house number where I spent the first 18 years of my life, and then it turned out that 617 is also the area code for Boston, where I spent the longest period of my career. Overall, the numbering of Monette trumpets conveys a sense of continuity.

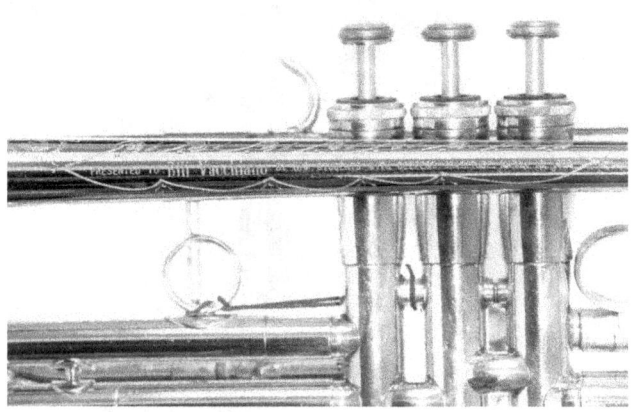

#130, presented to Bill Vacchiano by his students on March 16, 1986 at the New York Brass Conference. Years later, Bill had sold it to a jazz player, who then tried to resell it on eBay. I made the winning bid and bought it directly—for nostalgic reasons. It's a terrific instrument, but of course Bill never used it in the New York Philharmonic, because he had retired almost 15 years before we gave it to him.

third intermission

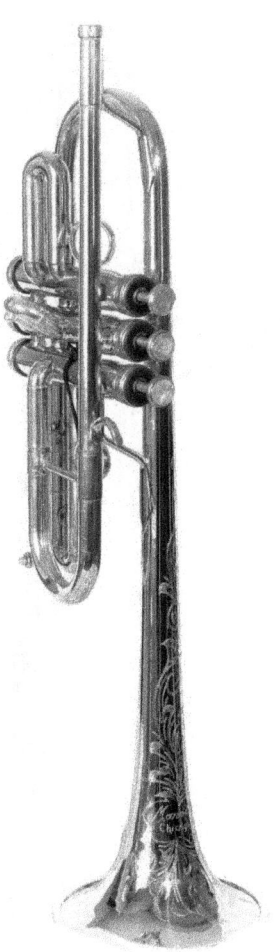

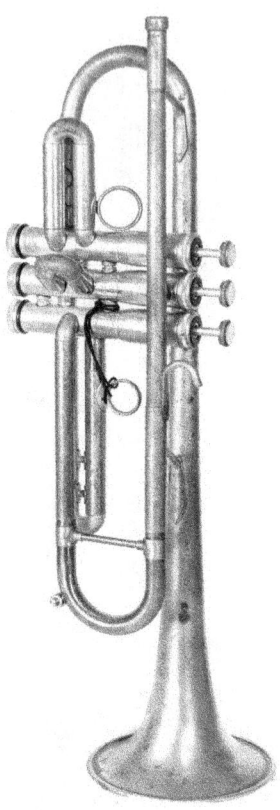

Dave Monette made this B-flat, #188, for a performance of Shostakovich's Piano Concerto No. 1 in C minor for Piano, Trumpet, and String Orchestra at Tanglewood in 1986, the first time the BSO had ever programmed it. Throughout my career, I played C trumpet almost exclusively, but a B-flat trumpet is necessary for a trumpet solo in the second movement of this great work.

Posthorn for Mozart's Serenade in D major, K. 320. The posthorn solo is usually played on trumpet, but Dave thought it would be fun to make this. I first played the piece with Seiji Ozawa and later with both Colin Davis and James Levine.

Posthorn for Mahler's Third Symphony. Dave made this for the performance of Mahler 3 that comprised James Levine's BSO audition.

Appendix

Essays from Students, Colleagues, and Friends

David Bamonte
*Assistant Principal Trumpet, Oregon Symphony;
Associate Professor, Portland State University*

What can I say about Charlie that hasn't already been said? To me he has been a teacher, mentor, confidant, and above all, a dear friend. His dedication to expanding the boundaries of what it means to be a musician and an artist has been a source of inspiration to me and other students of the trumpet all around the world. The playing concepts that I learned from Charlie were revolutionary to my playing and have been the source of any success that I have had throughout my career. But more than that, his philosophies on how to survive in this business have proven invaluable time and again. Some of our most impactful lessons happened not in his studio, but over a slice of pizza or a plate of Thai food. I am proud to have been able to pass along his teachings to my own students.

I first met Charlie 38 summers ago, at the 1983 International Trumpet Guild conference in Ithaca, New York. I was immediately struck by his sound, which was, at times, powerful and dominating but also lyric and incredibly *dolce* when needed. A truly unique sound. So, no surprise, when it came time for me to apply to graduate school, the New England Conservatory was at the top of my list.

My time studying with Charlie at NEC saw its ups and downs. During that first fall together, he spent our lessons bringing me back from the edge of despair. The previous summer I had tried to simultaneously learn Bach's *B Minor Mass* and the *Brandenburg Concerto #2* on a new piccolo trumpet and had managed to twist myself into such a knot of tension that I could hardly play. Looking back, perhaps this was a blessing in disguise. Having reached such a low point, I was ready to start from scratch, and Charlie spent many hours patiently reteaching me how to breathe, how to create an effortless sound, and how to mentally endure when times are hard. Within a couple of months, I was playing the best I ever had and had become a lifelong believer in Charlie's teachings.

Over the next few years I spent time with Charlie at both NEC and Tanglewood. His concepts were different from other well-known teachers at the time, yet the positive results were undeniable. His approach slowly became my approach, and I have done my best to pass on what I learned during my student days.

But things were not always so serious during lessons. One interaction in particular sticks out in my mind. I had prepared a Walter Smith *Top Tones* etude and, in the course of playing it, managed to screw up a passage, which I often did. Charlie took my horn to demonstrate and made the exact same mistake I had just made. Brushing that aside, he played the passage again ... and made the same mistake, again. On his third attempt, there it was, the *same mistake*. With a slight grin, he handed the trumpet back to me and said simply, "Go on." This humility is indicative of his teaching spirit; never one to tear down, even while maintaining the highest standards for his studio.

After school I was fortunate to become a colleague of Charlie's, and I played with the Boston Symphony Orchestra (BSO) as a substitute for 12 years. Although I was no longer a student, the learning never ceased. I can recall many "lessons" in the section of the BSO, where I was able to hear and internalize his sound on some of the greatest orchestral repertoire. I learned how to be a professional during these years, how to maintain my composure under pressure while still projecting thoughtful and emotionally driven performances. Three concerts from these years left a lasting impression: a performance of Mahler's *Symphony No. 5* at Carnegie Hall (a place where Charlie always seemed to play especially well), Mahler's *Symphony No. 2* with Seiji Ozawa in Cologne (while on a European tour with the BSO), and a Tuesday night performance of Bruckner's *Symphony No. 8* with Bernard Haitink in Symphony Hall. While there are almost too many concerts to remember, these three stand out as supreme examples of masterful trumpet playing; nights that I will never forget.

My only regret throughout my career has been that I haven't been able to see and hear Charlie as often as I did in my formative years. But I can solidly rely on my memories of his advice through the years to right the ship when things go south.

Eric M. Berlin

Professor, University of Massachusetts at Amherst;
Principal Trumpet, Albany Symphony Orchestra

Coming from a small town in Lancaster County, PA, I knew little of Charlie Schlueter, but WITF, the public radio station in Hershey, PA, played a live "big 5" orchestra concert each weekday evening. Here I first cocked my ear, as RCA's dog Nipper to "His Master's Voice."

Nowhere else had I heard the breadth of color, dynamic, and expressive range that came through my radio on BSO nights. With only that sound to guide me, I came to NEC to study with Charlie. That sound, a beacon calling me to Boston, continues to illuminate my path over 30 years later.

Fortunately, during my four years of school I heard *every* program the BSO played while working as an usher. Every concert was an education unto itself, Charlie's concepts in practice projecting to the very back of the hall. There, I heard his absolute commitment to the music, and a palette of colors I could never have imagined. Spectacular heroic performances of Mahler, Strauss, and Bruckner, of course, dominated the fascination of a young orchestral trumpeter wannabe, but Charlie's delicacy in French repertoire was particularly impressive. I remember every performance which went into the recordings of *Daphnis et Chloé* with Bernard Haitink and *Elektra* with Christa Ludwig. I will never forget the *Don Juan* solo with the strings in the slowest imaginable performance under Giuseppe Sinopoli. Charlie began as a mere whisper of deep purple in the string sound, gradually transforming into brilliant colors of red and orange to send the melody soaring into the audience.

Charlie's teaching approach was unique, and I use the same approach with my own students. In guided practice sessions, in the present and without judgement, Charlie guided us through the discovery of each new etude. He delivered universal concepts, applicable to all music, which brought us deeper inside the music to the intention of the composer, the nuance of the phrase, and which opened up infinite possibilities for personal expression beyond the obvious musical choice. The beauty of his conceptual approach is that it is as effective for the dozens of K–12 students I taught, straight out of college, as it is for the college students I now teach and for teaching myself at ever finer levels of detail.

Memories of lessons with Charlie are pleasantly infused with the sweet aroma of his pipe and coffee and mystery about why things worked. Only after several years of teaching myself did I realize how much he relied on indirection and distraction to get me out of my own way and realize my potential.

After one particularly frustrating week, I came in with "Charlie, I don't know what is wrong, my face feels terrible ..." and before I could continue, he exclaimed "Just shut up and play! Nobody is paying you to feel good." Shocking, and more forceful than I was used to, it was exactly what I needed to rearrange my brain cells.

In my first Albany Symphony season, our music director programmed what I thought was a once-in-a-lifetime concert of principal trumpet abuse: *Also Sprach* and *Planets*—*Planets* first (I would play the same program 15 years later with Ben Zander in Symphony Hall!). While playing for Charlie, I expressed how uncomfortable I was with all of the high C's. He slapped me on the leg and said, "When is the last time you worried about a high D on your B-flat trumpet in a big band?!"

It is impossible to overstate the impact of this simple question on my playing. In it, Charlie broke down the false barrier between my classical and commercial playing, allowing me to approach those notes with the freedom and joy I felt in my youth as a screamer, and it helped me to understand that the only impediment was my own mind.

After successfully negotiating an etude with Charlie's constant insistence on a single concept, he patted me on the back and exclaimed, "If I could tattoo one thing inside your eyelids, it would be 'end of the note!'" This single concept is perhaps the strongest part of my own teaching as it contains so much information. Years later, I received a text message on Christmas Eve from one of my most successful students: "I just wanted to let you know that I just played three Christmas services staying engaged through the end of every note."

As a teacher, small messages like this are meaningful validations of the impact we make. I immediately forwarded it to Charlie, as proof that his concepts remain strong through the ever-widening web of influence his teaching has had on his students and endless generations of those to come. With this book that we have all been waiting several decades for finally in print, the wider world will be able to benefit from this most inspired musician, who just happened to play trumpet. Thanks, Charlie!

Norman Bolter
Second Trombone, Boston Symphony Orchestra, and Principal Trombone, Boston Pops Orchestra (retired)

I remember 1972, Northrop Auditorium at the University of Minnesota. The Minnesota Orchestra was about to play Bruckner's *Symphony No. 4*. I noticed the new first trumpet player and was excited to hear him. Little did I know what I was in for!

My teachers were in the trombone section: Steven Zellmer, Ronald Ricketts, and Lawrence Weinman. I was anticipating their entrance. This is the orchestra I grew up with. This is the brass section I grew up with. Except for the new first trumpet player.

The piece started with principal hornist Robert Elworthy playing the opening solos very tastefully. The piece was starting to build in intensity and then—then I saw the new first trumpet player hold his horn up and take the most massive, open breath I had ever seen. But that was not the end of it. The sound emerged out of that horn and was all-encompassing. Totally three-dimensional—actually, at least four-dimensional! My jaw hit the ground every time the first trumpet came in!

That was my first experience hearing Charlie Schlueter. During his first season, I heard him do *Symphonie Fantastique*, the Hummel *Trumpet Concerto* and Mahler's *Symphony No. 3*. All were incredible.

Mahler's *Third Symphony* ... that left an impression on me that has still been unmatched by any player or performance I have heard since. I have heard great players play this amazing, ethereal posthorn solo but this—this literally was from another world. The phrasing, the sound, and the magnificent slurs were all integrated into an actual experience that produced a different state of being in myself. One entrance after another seemed to be more awe-inspiring. There was no doubt in my mind: I had experienced something truly special and unique.

When I moved to Boston the following year to start my short stint at New England Conservatory, I would always look forward to coming back to Minneapolis to hear Charlie and my teachers. Plus, the whole orchestra was home to top-notch artists on many instruments. I remember one of my times visiting home when I heard Bruckner 7 with Klaus Tennstedt. It was an extra exciting performance for me because my sixteen-year-old brother Neal was playing the low Wagner tuben part. Neal sounded unreal and, of course, so did Charlie and the whole orchestra. During that time, I also met Charlie at Chester E. Groth Music Company in downtown Minneapolis, in Paul Walton's repair shop. We had a good talk and, little did I know, eight years later we would both be playing in the Boston Symphony together!

Charlie's audition with the orchestra was head and shoulders above that of anyone else who auditioned. This, for me, marked the beginning of a different era in the BSO, but at the same time, it was fitting a format that the orchestra seemed to have followed for decades and that was to pick players who had unique features in their playing and who really went for the music.

This turned out to be the last era, in my mind, of going for it with the whole of you, dynamically and musically. I was so happy to have made wonderful orchestra recordings with Charlie of Mahler 5 and Mahler 7, plus wonderful performances of Bartók's *Concerto for Orchestra*, all the Strauss tone poems, *Poem of Ecstasy*, and all the great Wagner material from *Götterdämmerung*, just to name a few!

Charlie was never afraid to be his own person and artist and play the instrument he wanted. This quality, along with his strong loyalty, warmth, and honesty, is what I admire and love about Charlie. These qualities came out in his playing, his person, and also in his teaching.

I was also very excited to write pieces that were really for Charlie's artistry and character. Chief among them is *On the Cusp* for solo trumpet, brass ensemble, and percussion. I was very honored that Charlie put some of the pieces I wrote for him on a couple of his solo albums. The main reason I wrote these pieces was to give return for what Charlie has given me. Thanks, Charlie, for everything, and more importantly, for being yourself no matter what the odds were. That alone is something to learn and catch the way of.

Russ DeVuyst
Associate Principal Trumpet, Montreal Symphony Orchestra (retired); Associate Professor, McGill University

At New England Conservatory of Music, between the years of 1983–1985, Charlie Schlueter guided me in my Master of Music program in trumpet studies of orchestral repertoire, musicality, trumpet techniques, and the art of "$#%& 'em if they can't take a joke" philosophy. I loved it. Finally, someone who was "real" without bullshit; a lay-it-on-the-line approach to "the way it should go" concept.

I took lessons with as many teachers as I could during my undergraduate and graduate years in Boston and do not suggest that any of these teachers were less than experts in their field. I learned much from many and incorporated those experiences gained from them into my own personality. Every teacher I studied with had an effect on me, but there were some that made lasting impressions.

Charlie was unique in his approach to teaching and showed me what could be done with music, and especially with orchestral excerpts. I remember one incident when I was playing a piece in the orchestral repertoire, possibly Mahler, and he explained how the phrase was constructed and where one could put an emphasis on certain notes to bring out the phrase to let it say all it had to. My reaction was, "You can do that in this music?" as if it was taboo to do anything else but play the notes exactly with perfect tone, intonation, precise articulation and rhythm, in strict time with ultimate consistency, driving the notes to their destination of boredom and ultimate doom!

Charlie was all about finding the essence of the music and going to the limits of it. The "just playing the notes" concept had no place in his vocabulary. In this sense, he taught you to be aware of what each note had in relation to the next note, the micro phrase and the main phrase, forming it into a common-sense musical entity that had substance, life, excitement, creativity, and joy. It wasn't about getting each note perfectly. It was about the ultimate outcome of the music and the freedom to express just that. Just trying to get the notes gets in the way of making music. It creates restriction, tension, worry, and insecurity, driving one to a downward spiral of inadequacy. Instead, you were encouraged to feel free to make mistakes, missed notes, clams! This freedom to "clam" releases all the insecurities that one places upon oneself and opens one up to playing the music without restrictions. Consequently, with this philosophy I missed fewer notes because I didn't concern myself with "just notes." It became difficult to miss a note. I was too concerned with how I was going to shape or articulate it to fit the musical idea that I'd formulated in my mind and with the general style of the overall piece I was playing.

He was also good at calming the mind and had techniques that were out of the ordinary. There was a psychological approach to keeping the mind busy to focus on what was needed without distraction.

Deciding to do a master's degree after a trumpet hiatus of two years or less and a period of six or seven years since my bachelor's degree was a challenge that brought insecurities, since I would ultimately be the oldest student in school. The 25-year-old master's students would constantly and unsuccessfully inquire about my age as if the five- or six-year gap made such a difference. Even though I had managed to win an audition with the Rhode Island Philharmonic, I still had much to learn. One day during a lesson, Charlie expressed that I was older and therefore somewhat set in my playing style. This actually shocked me, and I retorted that I was flexible to change into whatever I wanted. That I was actually without style and trying to find some sort of stability and security in the realm of orchestral music since I had such limited knowledge of it. Sure, I could play it, but why was *Petrouchka* so difficult? And *Pictures at an Exhibition*—what made that so difficult? It was just quarter notes with a couple of eighth notes stuck in. And why did I keep screwing up Schumann *Symphony No. 2*? With these excerpts, and others we went through, it became clear, and a simple common-sense approach took hold. I didn't split the high G in Schumann *Symphony No. 2* anymore, and could play it softly with a free and unrestricted tone. *Petrouchka* became simple, with the micro phrases it contained, and flowed gracefully in the dance-like manner it was intended to. It was locked into my psyche. I was relieved.

But perhaps the story that I refer to most often was when I was actually invited to take an audition for a big orchestra and had one week to get an audition together. I called Charlie in a panic and told him. He had a calm disposition and asked me what the list was. I started to list the excerpts. *Pictures* "Promenade" and "Goldenberg and Schmuyle." He said, "Well, I heard you play that and you sounded good. What else?" I blurted, "*Pines of Rome*, opening and offstage solo; Mahler 5, first movement; *Petrouchka*, Dance and Waltz and piccolo part at the end; *Carmen, Ein Heldenleben, American in Paris,* Mahler 3 ..." and the list went on. With every excerpt mentioned, he said, "I heard you play that, and you sounded good." The next question was, "Well, what do I do?" And he said, "Don't practice. If you start practicing, you'll ruin your chops, they will swell up and when you get to the audition, you won't be able to play." I took his advice, but only at 80%. I had to brush up on a few things that were questionable. However, that taught me to trust in what I had worked on to be good and to trust in myself. Once you know something, it is yours. All you have to do is trust that you do know it. It was by far one of the best auditions I've played. I felt in control and confident. I didn't get the gig, but it didn't matter. I knew what to do now. I went on to win principal in the Memphis Symphony, and associate principal in Montreal, as well as principal in Israel. Thanks, Charlie.

Mireia Farres
*Solo Trumpet, Barcelona Symphony Orchestra;
Professor, Catalonia College of Music*

Me and Charlie ...

My first meeting with Charlie wasn't quite normal. Let me explain: I'm from Barcelona and I got my trumpets stolen in a bus when I was coming from a trumpet course in France. I decided to fly to New York and Boston to buy new trumpets. Since I was 17 and wanted to study with Charlie (because of a Mahler 5 recording that I totally fell in love with), I thought it would be a great idea to go to New York, get the trumpets, and then fly to Boston to meet Charlie for a lesson and take a look at New England Conservatory. I did that. The only problem was that once I got to New York, I went to every single store and couldn't find any trumpets that I liked, so I had to call Charlie and tell him that I had no trumpets to play in my lesson the next day. As nice and gentle as he always is, he told me that it wasn't a problem. He would bring me to a store right before the lesson and I would be able to find a good trumpet. The next day, we met at Rayburn, and he had already picked some B-flat and C trumpets for me. I saw him outside the store with his pipe and his cup of coffee in his hands. He smiled at me and we went inside the shop. He gave me a C11 Monette mouthpiece to try and asked me to play scales up to high C and above to start. Then he looked at me and said, "You'll be fine with that, let's find you some trumpets to start on." That took us about one hour at most, and then we went to NEC for the lesson.

Once we entered his studio, I smelled that coffee/pipe aroma that will always remind me of him, and I knew I was going to study with him. I picked up my new B-flat trumpet and told him I was going to play Hindemith. Once again, he looked at me and he said, "Why don't you just play it on your new C trumpet?" I thought in my head, "WHAT???" In my first class with that amazing human being, who happened to be the BSO principal trumpet, he was already asking me to work with my brain rather than with my lips!!!! After that, a great relationship developed over my three years studying with him.

I always happened to have my lesson late in the afternoon. It was his last lesson after a long day of rehearsals and classes, and he was hungry—I knew that because all the comparisons he made would somehow be about food, telling me that I had to play that staccato like spaghetti *al dente* (a saying I now use with my students).

There are many, many things I can say about Charlie and "the end of the note," but most importantly, I love how he made me discover a whole world of sounds and how to project them through the trumpet: the way he made me think and the way he worked on my brain to understand that this issue was the beginning of the whole playing process.

In one of our lessons, I was concerned about taking time off without losing my abilities. He told me that over summer break, he would take some weeks off and that he would be able to start again with Mahler, if that was required. I was in shock—*how was he able to do that?* His answer: "When I take the trumpet again, I just think that it was yesterday that I played. I don't think that I have taken some days off. It's all in your head and you know how to get it back if you know how you want it." After that I thought that the most important thing is to know exactly how you want to sound—like in every moment—and let your brain and body do the rest.

I love him so much. We became almost family; he's Uncle Charlie for my three kids and, even if we go one month without talking, I know he's there for me and he knows I'm there for him. I feel so lucky that life brought us together and that his music and sound called me to go to Boston and meet him.

I've always thought that he was ahead of his time and that his sound will be always timeless. It is so relaxed, so present, and so rich—it's a sound with a great soul. Time went by and I'm now 36 with three children, I have a principal position in the Barcelona Symphony, and I'm so thankful for that. I just wish I wasn't too far away from him to smell that coffee every now and then and have nice conversations over some chili.

Thank you so much for everything you gave me and for all that music that filled me up so many times. I love you, Charlie!

Tim Hudson

Associate Professor, Gardner-Webb University;
Founder and Leader, Carolina Brass

When Charlie asked me to write a little on how his teachings have influenced my performing and teaching career, my reply was I wasn't sure if I had time to write a book as well! But, I'll be as brief as possible, given the fact that his teaching and playing continue to inspire me even as I write this, and as I move forward with my own career of teaching and performing. Going back to the late 1980s, I attended NEC for an MM in Trumpet performance solely to study with Charlie. I had never met him, talked to him or heard him live, but hearing his recordings with the BSO were so intriguing that I had to know what he was doing to get "that sound" and "that articulation." It was different. And to my ears, far superior to most any other playing I had ever heard. My studies with Charlie resulted in the most rapid growth possible as a musician and trumpet player. These concepts that have immensely helped me which I continue to pass along to my students include the following: inhaling to the fullest capacity, shaping notes, relaxing, using slow hot air, maximum resonance with minimum intensity, pushing the slide in and keeping the pitch down, posture/body alignment and awareness, finding a musical solution to solve a seemingly technical/mechanical problem, note grouping, staying in the present, broadening out the sound north south east west, dealing with the color of the sound, and the list goes on ... My students currently hold positions such as Los Angeles Philharmonic Second Trumpet, Houston Symphony Associate Principal Trumpet and Charlotte Symphony Principal (at age 21!), shows on Broadway, The Glenn Miller Orchestra, former Principal Trumpet Mexico City Philharmonic, university professors, etc. This is all a result of the teachings of Charlie Schlueter, which I have the privilege of passing along to my students.

Rod MacDonald
Former Principal Trumpet, Leipzig Gewandhaus Orchestra; Music Director, New England Symphony Orchestra

I was one of five trumpet students in the fellowship student orchestra at Tanglewood in 1982. Then called the Berkshire Music Center Orchestra, we had just arrived for a great summer of music-making. Charles Schlueter also had just arrived to start his new position as principal trumpet of the Boston Symphony. I then fantasized this was the best position to have in North America. The long tradition of the BSO and the summer season in the Berkshires of Massachusetts playing orchestral music seemed ideal. I couldn't imagine anything better. The five of us had heard about Mr. Schlueter. Of all the rumors, we, of course, gravitated to the one where he could play the loudest. Or at least could play above the orchestra better than anyone on the continent. Being new-lings, this was, of course, a very impressive attribute. We would give a nod to all the other wonderful aspects of Mr. Schlueter's playing, but this seemed to stick out most in our minds. Our first meeting was our initial master class with Mr. Schlueter on a warm, sunny midday outside a wooden building where mosquitoes had found their way in overnight but had not yet escaped during the morning. We were standing outside the hut, and Charlie came down the path in the woods. A man of a young age ... maybe 40? I could look this up, but I think I will stay on my path for the moment here. He had, then, the same haircut and open shirt with the beads around his neck that he still prefers today. The beads looked like they were from the '60s, I think (or at least that's my guess). Since it was warm, he wore an open dress shirt, though in the cold winter months in Boston he would have his turtleneck and again with the beads. His smile and greeting immediately took the trepidation out of the first encounter. He bowed his head slightly down, looking up to meet our eyes as we shook hands. It kind of reminded me of someone that might have spent some serious time in Japan.

For those who have not visited, posture, body language, and humility play a big role in Japan. Being an American in America, Mr. Schlueter had no need for any show of humility in his body language—neither would any of us expect this. It was there, nevertheless, and very disarming, and we were all quickly on a first-name basis. Well, Charlie taught our very first lesson as a group where he talked about his concepts of making music in the orchestra: consideration for the ends of the notes, full breath, tuning high, playing low, and so on. Anyone who has studied with Charlie knows what I'm talking about. So that was our first meeting. As a footnote, many of his concepts really didn't take until I had my job in the Gewandhaus Orchestra in Leipzig. It wasn't until I was quasi in the line of fire that many of the echoes of past lessons came to fruition. I recall times where I even believed I thought of it all myself, but I now recollect otherwise.

Charlie was my trumpet studio teacher during my master's degree at the New England Conservatory. Charlie, with a decade of BSO tenure behind him, taught in NEC's Jordan Hall (across the street from Symphony Hall), and we had the usual weekly lessons and trumpet studio class with him. During that time, Charlie would allow us to sneak into his BSO concerts. There were tickets available to students for Friday afternoon concerts, but they were limited. Usually there was a sign-up list on the Beethoven statue in the NEC lobby, where people with BSO subscriptions could donate tickets at the last minute so that the seats wouldn't remain empty. There were always a few tickets available, but when you didn't get a ticket and there was something of interest for a trumpet player on the program, Charlie, without any formality, came to the musicians' entrance to allow us in. It might have been Bartók *Concerto for Orchestra* or Mahler 3, it was always the same procedure: making sure his students could hear the live concerts. This was a creature comfort during my NEC studies and a perk that proves the best things in life are free. I generally stood in the back. There were only sporadic seats available and I thought standing in the back on the top balcony had the best sound.

I have clear recollection of the student trumpet studio critiquing Charlie's performances the day after. I remember how we would greet Charlie after one of his BSO performances the next day. It all seems totally impolite how we told him how he might have played a phrase or note differently. I now look back at our comments and feel we were impossibly unfair with our criticism. I remember hearing Mahler 5 and, the following day, telling him what I thought about how he might have played a passage differently. How the *Leonore* offstage trumpet "signal" could have been a bit so more or how he could have played a passage in a Bruckner symphony differently. I now can't believe how he was so cheerful for our comments. I remember saying it could have been more this or more that. Charlie would smile and simply make a comment to the effect of why he did it that way or he would just listen. I wasn't the only one to do this, too. If I came off stage after playing Mahler 5 in Leipzig and had a student run after me and tell me how it might have been better, I don't think I would have the patience or the kind words of encouragement. This, distinctly, is one of the Charlie moments I remember clearly: his humanity of standing above the whole picture, and how he enjoyed our outpouring of interest in wanting entrance in the exclusive club of classical orchestra musicians. And that's exactly how I believe he took it, too. Always the commensurate teacher and our music guru.

In December 1988, shortly before Herbert von Karajan died, the BSO was on tour in Germany and was scheduled to perform Mahler's *Ninth Symphony* in the Berlin Philharmonie. I must have had that night off to have gotten away from Leipzig performances. Another member of the orchestra (the horn player Roberto Minczuk from Brazil) and I rode the train to Berlin and made our way to the Philharmonie to hear the BSO and Ozawa with Charlie on lead. I actually think that von Karajan's death resulted in a cloud hanging over Berlin, and that the then-BSO music director was "pokering" to win the now-vacated top spot at the helm of Germany's flagship orchestra. Coming to Berlin with an orchestral chestnut like Mahler 9 was, of course, a provocative statement, too. The wolves were waiting at the door, and no one could possibly succeed the now-dead legend. Von Karajan was such a monumental figure in the orchestral world in Europe that it seemed to most that a new era had begun and an old one had ended. Mahler 9 is a work where the composer was realizing his own mortality, and it is a cornerstone of the great classical repertoire. It also has to be one of the most profound trumpet parts of the classical repertoire, with its dark and macabre burlesque and its angelic, stratospheric trumpet melodies and intervals in the slower movement. Simply said, after this long setup, it was some of the best trumpet playing, brass playing, and orchestral playing I have ever heard. Everyone was on their A game from far away New England. Charlie was leading the brass like I have never heard a section function. Such a tone center from the tuba on up. This performance with Charlie solidified all of the techniques and philosophy he taught us in our studio. It was here that I heard it all put together—what he was trying to teach us—the embodiment of the music transcending the constraints of a physical instrument. I will never forget that performance and it will remain indelibly in my memory as a stellar moment in live orchestral music. As I remember playing the same trumpet part and piece on tour, Charlie's performance was a benchmark for my inner ear.

Brian McCreath
Director of Production, WCRB/WGBH, Boston

Whenever I see Charlie Schlueter these days, more than 25 years since I was officially a student of his, we joke about the number of careers I've had. In reality the number is pretty low, but it's true that making a living as a trumpet player is only one of them. But no matter which career it's been, one constant is what I learned from Charlie.

It's hard to say what I needed most from a teacher in 1988, when I came to the New England Conservatory. It seems like a thousand different things were going on with me at the time, and if I were to look back and detail it all I would probably end up wanting to crawl under a rock. Maybe what I really needed was someone to make sense of the very accumulation of those thousand things, a heaping pile of bad habits, faulty techniques, and twisted approaches. And that was before even picking up a trumpet.

But pick up a trumpet was the first thing we did. It was, after all, the whole point of undertaking a degree program. I had been warned previously that, if I spent the following few months with my head swimming, questioning even those aspects of my playing that I thought were foundational, everything would be going according to plan. It's just how things worked with Charlie.

The subsequent months—during which, yes, my head was swimming, questioning even those aspects of my playing that I thought were foundational—might have been enough to get an early start on one of those other careers. But as it turned out, that time of recalibration, adjusting to a whole new set of parameters in how music worked its way into my ears, through my brain, and out my lips, fingers, and lungs, was the New Foundational. More importantly, what allowed that rebuilding of the foundation was the utter generosity, warmth, and support Charlie demonstrated in every single lesson and interaction.

That's right: the person who dismantled everything I was doing wrong, along with everything I thought I was doing right, was also the one who reassured me that the musician at the core of it all—me—possessed validity and possibility. And with that reassurance, new parameters were established, new process was built, and a transformed framework of understanding music took hold.

Along the way, Charlie's compassionate mentorship made my lessons with him something quite a bit more than trumpet lessons. There was no doubt that most of my fellow NEC students had good relationships with their teachers. But it always felt (and still feels) like those of us who studied with Charlie were learning something extra, beyond the etudes and the excerpts, something like a lens through which to see life.

After I left NEC I played professionally for several years, teaching along the way. I put my best efforts into being as warm and generous as Charlie with my own students. And as a performer, I was fortunate to play with several other former students of Charlie's—who knew instantly what the end of the note is all about—and many others for whom the end of the note has no meaning. It was Charlie's teaching that made it possible to thrive in both scenarios. It didn't matter who I was performing with, I adapted through that framework of hearing. As I moved into other careers, first in artist management and then in radio, that same framework has remained vital.

Amazingly, after a series of twists and turns, near misses and unexpected opportunities, I've found myself back where Charlie spent two and a half decades teaching by example: Symphony Hall in Boston. As the producer of WCRB's Boston Symphony Orchestra radio broadcasts, I'm not only privileged to hear that extraordinary orchestra on a constant basis. I also get to tell the stories from the present and the past that make the BSO such a distinctive orchestra. In the process, the recordings of the orchestra during the '80s and '90s serve as a vivid reminder that I was equally privileged earlier in my life, when Charlie Schlueter's wisdom and generosity made all the difference.

Jimi Michel
Global and Digital Health Consultant

"We've got trouble in Botswana!"

It was my first day on the job as a global health consultant, and I hadn't even finished my HR paperwork, when someone ran into the room to announce that there had been a major data collection error in one of our African programs. At the time, I didn't know where Botswana was (some very sheepish Googling revealed that it's just above South Africa), and I had no prior knowledge of the program, but I took a deep breath and then my mind was off—*How big was the original sample size? Would we have to recollect everything or would a smaller, supplemental survey work? Does Botswana have a rainy season that we'll need to worry about?*

My coursework in global health and epidemiology from Boston University served me well that day, but my three years studying with Charlie Schlueter served me even better. Data loss in a country you've never heard of is one thing, but it doesn't seem so bad after going into your first lesson with the principal trumpet of the Boston Symphony and trying to sight-read the etude in D-sharp minor from Walter Smith's *Top Tones*!

Charlie was well-known for having students sight-read at every lesson, but it was more than just sight-reading. Although lessons touched on everything from rhythm and intonation to phrasing and dynamics, they were really about developing a framework for playing the instrument and making music. Later, after I'd shifted my professional focus away from music, I realized that his lessons applied well beyond the instrument or music in general. Using Charlie's conceptual approach has allowed me to sight-read *anything*, from orchestral excerpts to computer code.

Charlie's discography is extensive, but those recordings pale in comparison to the memories I have of his live performances. A performance of Sibelius 2 at Symphony Hall stands out for the way he led the brass section in the final movement with a balance of power and grace that only he could produce. Most remarkably, though, in my mind are the memories of his soft playing, like the opening moments of *La Mer* or the muted arpeggios at the end of the opening movement of Mahler 5—in those moments, Charlie played so softly but also with such *presence* and *resonance* that it seemed almost *implied*, as if the sound barely existed, yet filled the hall with warmth.

Charlie—for those memories, and for all of the lessons that I use every day, and for your enduring support and friendship, I say *Thank You*!

David G. Monette
Founder, David G. Monette Corporation

It would be impossible to overstate the influence Charlie Schlueter has had on the world of brass instrument performance and pedagogy. With his holistic, visionary approach, Charlie has blown apart conventions in not only how the trumpet sounds and is played ... but also how playing the trumpet is taught. Those who enjoy revolutionary musicianship have loved experiencing Charlie's fearless approach to music-making—an approach Charlie has embraced and in which he has thrived. His exceptional ability to weave through the orchestral fabric with unheard-of layers of both subtle nuance and masterful aplomb with colleagues such as Phil Myers, Buddy Wright, Chester Schmitz, and Norm Bolter (to name just a few) have brought out new musical dimensions in familiar works that have inspired audiences and his pupils worldwide for over four decades. His most recent solo CD—with three new world premiere pieces written for him that exceed the abilities of trumpet mortals—is a perfect example of how he also embraces visionary contemporary music.

Charlie's very presence onstage has meant that previous limits in blending, phrasing, and dynamic extremes were left behind. His exceptional virtuosity has provided so many of us with countless musical highs in times where these experiences are becoming increasingly rare. In some orchestral situations, careful, note-perfect performances have become more important than taking the kinds of musical chances previous generations have enjoyed. Charlie Schlueter never shies away from cutting-edge spontaneity and excitement! In my work as an instrument maker, among my biggest influences have been Charlie, Maynard, and Wynton. These three players have shaped my own career by example—inspiring the most innovative new Monette instrument designs over the last 35 years. It is no exaggeration to say that without Charlie's profound influence, Monette instruments would likely not exist today.

Charlie's expanded dynamic range from whisper tones to *fffff*—and everything in between—is unparalleled. I am reminded of meeting Charlie and Wynton at Hal Oringer's studio in lower Manhattan right after they both received their first sheet-braced RAJA instruments—the first Monette C and Bb trumpets with integral mouthpieces. Wynton played for Charlie first. The depth and clarity were unlike anything either of us had heard before. Then Charlie picked up his new C trumpet and played the opening of Mahler 5 for us ... with a sound that Gustav Mahler probably heard from the grave! Wynton—in his own humble way—just walked over to his case, shook his head, put his horn away and said he needed to go home and practice!

Several times Charlie and I went out to hear Maynard and the band at top jazz clubs. Maynard loved having Charlie visit—particularity the "hang" before the show started. "Boss" would always ask Charlie to play a few notes for him in the dressing room. Maynard would sit with his eyes closed ... taking in the warmth and resonance of this rare trumpet peer.

Charlie's radical approach to playing and teaching has been influenced by his own version of various holistic mind/body practices he incorporates onstage and in his teaching studio. He has spent his life studying and living the work of Milton Erickson, Eloise Ristad, and (most recently) Moshe Feldenkrais, among others. As this is being written, Charlie—at age 79—has recently completed the first two years of Feldenkrais Practitioner training. This devotion to his own personal evolution and growth is just one more example of how he sets the highest standards for his pupils, worldwide, to follow. As a fearless innovator himself, Charlie always encouraged my own innovations. I remember back in the mid-80s sometime, I had just completed the first Monette C trumpet mouthpiece. The BSO was playing a Mahler symphony right then, and despite a blizzard slowing down air travel, I made it to the stage door twenty minutes before curtain. Charlie immediately asked to try this new, totally unproven mouthpiece. At first, I balked, but he talked me into letting him try it right there at the stage door. He played half a dozen notes, said he liked it, then took it onstage and played the entire performance on it. He never looked back. How fortunate for me to have this level of trust in a friend and client supporting me to the extreme! Charlie's approach to both playing and teaching has been so far ahead of his time that he has left a legacy that, in some circles, could be misunderstood. Thankfully, this book—over three decades in the making—will answer many questions and provide insight for those who want to better understand the essence of his revolutionary approach. Thank you, my dear friend Charlie Schlueter, for all you have done to inspire so many of us in the unique ways only you can.

Lester P. Monts
Professor and Senior Vice Provost Emeritus for Academic Affairs, University of Michigan

What an honor it is for me to reminisce about one of the most exciting periods of my life as a trumpet player—my years of study with Charlie Schlueter. Over a fifteen-year period (1965–1980), I studied with eight different trumpet teachers. My major teachers were Robert Bright, 1965–1969 at Arkansas Tech University; Dennis Schneider, 1970–1972 at the University of Nebraska; and, of course, Charlie Schlueter, 1975–1979 at the University of Minnesota. Even though my work life has shifted from trumpet player to ethnomusicologist to academic administrator, the trumpet is forever a part of my soul. Charlie Schlueter instilled in me an artistic spirit and work ethic that has been with me for more than forty years.

After completing my master's degree in trumpet performance at Nebraska in 1972, I sought to continue my studies with a player in one of the "Big Five" orchestras. After a few inquiries, Dennis Schneider suggested that I check out Charlie Schlueter. At the time, Charlie was assistant principal in the Cleveland Orchestra. I had heard great things about his teaching and had learned about the success of one of his star students. When an opening for a studio trumpet teacher was announced at Edinboro University (PA), I auditioned and won the position. Edinboro is located eighty-five miles northwest of Cleveland, a reasonable driving distance to hear the orchestra and to study with Charlie.

Just before the move to Edinboro in 1972, Charlie moved to Minneapolis to assume the principal job with the Minnesota Orchestra. This was a real disruption to my plans. Over the next three years, Charlie's legacy was still very much alive in the Cleveland area. I managed to study with one of his former students, who taught using Charlie's philosophy. By 1975, I was not making the progress I desired, so I decided to take a leave of absence from Edinboro University to begin doctoral studies at the University of Minnesota where Charlie also served as a professor of trumpet. At the time, Minnesota did not offer a Doctor of Musical Arts degree in trumpet performance, so I enrolled in the graduate program in ethnomusicology, my newfound area of interest. I did not know, at the time, that Charlie could only take a limited number of students, so when I initially contacted him, he said that, due to his schedule with the orchestra, it was doubtful he could take on another student. I was thoroughly distraught. Here I was on leave from my position at Edinboro, recently married, and without confirmation to act on the real reason I was in Minneapolis. A few days later, Charlie called and said he had an opening. Hurray! I studied with Charlie over the next four years, except the time I spent in Liberia, West Africa, conducting ethnomusicological field research.

Before my studies with Charlie, I played with the Lincoln and Omaha Symphony Orchestras, the Omaha opera and ballet orchestras, the Erie Philharmonic, and started a fifteen-year stint as principal trumpet with the Allegheny

Music Festival and the Music Festival of Arkansas. I even played the Telemann Concerto with the Pittsburgh Symphony during their residency on the campus at Edinboro. With all that behind me, it was Charlie who introduced me to the big time! He graciously arranged for me to play utility trumpet jobs with the Minnesota Orchestra, the Minnesota Opera Orchestra, and the St. Paul Chamber Orchestra. My greatest thrills with the Minnesota Orchestra were performing the Berlioz *Requiem* and the Khachaturian *Symphony No. 3* with 15 trumpets. On another occasion during a lesson, Charlie asked if I could play a gig with the St. Paul Chamber Orchestra, saying, "It should be an easy blow." This turned out to be the pinnacle of my performance career. I arrived at the rehearsal and Aaron Copland (my favorite American composer) stepped to the podium! I later asked Charlie why he didn't tell me that Copland was conducting that concert. He said, "I didn't want to scare you off."

As a result of Charlie's masterful tutelage, I became a much more confident trumpet player, which has contributed to my success in many phases of my professional life over the years. My most challenging performance roles occurred when I served as principal trumpet for orchestras at the Allegheny Summer Music Festival and the Music Festival of Arkansas. Each summer, conductor Carlton Woods selected heavily trumpet-ridden literature from the orchestral and chamber repertoire. As a beneficiary of Charlie's understanding of the orchestral literature and his substantive pedagogical skills, I approached the performance challenges with the utmost confidence.

Another memorable experience with Charlie that contributed to my musical development was when he said that "trumpet music is music!" By that he meant there are patterns in music that, once understood, make trumpet playing understandable. Like his teacher, Bill Vacchiano,

Charlie tried to instill a healthy attitude about music. At one of my lessons, I was sight-reading an etude and kept stumbling over a repeated arpeggiated passage. Charlie said, "Come on, it's just an ascending diminished 7th chord." Having studied with six previous trumpet teachers, no one had ever made such a reference as part of a lesson. Charlie then asked me to play the notes of a diminished 7th chord starting on D-flat. I was so startled by the suggestion that I timidly attempted to do so. Charlie said, "How did you get this far and not know that?" Well, I was actually a very good music theory student and was totally embarrassed that I didn't make the connection at that moment. That episode turned out to be one of my best lessons. From then on, not only did I look for and identify similar patterns in my own playing, I made it an important part of my teaching.

As an African American, I will always appreciate Charlie's approach to diversity and inclusion. Throughout the time I studied with him, I always believed he had my best interests at heart. While things are not so different today for African American orchestral musicians, back then Charlie was an encouraging voice, urging me to take auditions and providing me opportunities to gain the much-needed experience to move to the next level in the profession. I certainly wasn't one of Charlie's top students, but once I gained his confidence as a committed player, he went out of his way to advance my development. When I completed the requirements for the PhD, I confidently applied for teaching positions in studio trumpet and ethnomusicology. Before I was offered a faculty position at the University of California, Santa Barbara, Charlie told me about an American Symphony Orchestra League program to increase the number of minorities in the nation's symphony orchestras. I will be forever grateful that he was willing to nominate me for a year-long internship with a major symphony orchestra.

My personal relationship with Charlie was very much like that which I had with my two other major teachers, Robert Bright and Dennis Schneider. Charlie was a teacher, a confidant, and a friend for whom I continue to have the utmost respect. In ethnomusicological circles, he would be considered a *guru*, or as the Vai people of Liberia would say, a trumpet *manja*, or trumpet chief. While studying with Charlie, I was a member of a cadre of devoted students who engaged in a sort of hero worship. I often joined groups of students who sat together in the balcony at Orchestra Hall so that we would have an unobstructed view of Charlie. Attending those concerts was very much a part of our training, and we were always inspired hearing Charlie play.

I've attended major orchestra concerts throughout the U.S., Europe, and Asia. I've heard many exceedingly gifted orchestral trumpet players, including Adolph Herseth, Bernard Adelstein, William Vacchiano, Gilbert Johnson, Armando Ghitalla, and many others. Charlie Schlueter is certainly a part of this distinguished group of principal trumpet players. But because of his contributions to my musical and personal life, I will always place him at the top of that list.

Barry Perkins
Principal Trumpet, Pacific Symphony;
Hollywood studio recording artist

First off, I would like to say that the little time I had with Charlie Schlueter changed my playing and my life forever. When I first came to the New England Conservatory, I was one of those players that could play high, fast, and muscle things around. My thoughts were that if I just do more of that and learn more repertoire, I would have a promising career. Boy was I wrong. In Charlie's studio, I found myself around a lot of other trumpet players that could do the same thing, but there was something different. It was one thing to shine amongst your fellow high school trumpet players, but yet another to play with college players that had good pitch centers and big orchestral sounds. Not only was my sound apparently not getting past the violins, I found that my endurance was suffering in quintet and small ensembles. So there you have it. Muscling things around was just not working at this level, so I had to figure out what was going on and fix it somehow.

During lessons with Charlie, I learned that, for starters, I needed to push in my tuning slide (which was out a mile) and play down on the pitch. I was determined to find the colors in the sound that Charlie and the others in his studio seemed to have. Another thing was that I discovered I wasn't using enough air in the right way. I never even thought about breathing, or playing where the horn resonates, before that point. All of this was uncharted territory and very exciting to me. He taught me simply to play on the right part of the sound so I could hear those colors and get them to reach the back of the hall.

After months of practicing in this more relaxed manner and opening up my ears, things started to settle in. I started to feel where the notes lay naturally on my horn and learned to play more on the center of the pitch and to the corners of the room. This opened up the upper register and increased my endurance dramatically. Needless to say, I was convinced.

In the short time that I was there, and, aside from helping me with my approach to the trumpet, Charlie had me sight-read quite a bit. Again, this was something I needed to do. I would ask him about certain excerpts, and he always blew me away with new information only a master orchestral player could know. It was so long ago that I don't remember specifics, but I do remember that I loved asking him questions and listening to the answers. It would be years later in my own orchestra, playing a Mahler symphony, when something would come up musically that I remember he said to listen for. It was pretty amazing the pearls of wisdom he would lay on me as a student that I truly didn't understand until years later in the orchestra.

Charlie seemed to sense that I was a starving student, not only for knowledge, but for food as well. Many times, I had the last lesson slot, and after the lesson, he would take me to the pizza place on the corner and order a large pizza pie. He would want only one piece and somehow the rest of the pizza ended up in my stomach. After dinner and virtually every chance I could get, I would make my way into Boston Symphony concerts and listen to Charlie demonstrate what he talked about in every lesson. This was more valuable than anything else I learned in Boston. To see the concepts in action and feel the goose bumps as Charlie's sound would reach the back of the hall where I was standing was something I will never forget. He played with a soulfulness that I'd never heard before.

It was definitely divine intervention that I ended up studying with Charlie, because without that experience, I wouldn't be the player I am today. It's hard to believe that just after a year at the Conservatory, I was able to win my first orchestra job at the age of 20. At the time of writing this, it has been almost 27 years since I studied with him and those pearls of wisdom still seem to bring on new meaning every time one of those symphonies comes across the stand. One of the greatest compliments I ever received came from a violist in the front of the orchestra who said my sound was like getting a powerful velvet hug from the back row. I realized in that moment that, not only do I hear the colors, but the orchestra appreciates them, too. This beats orchestra members ducking for cover any day! In short, whether it is sight-reading on a recording session for a major motion picture or waiting to peg the high D's in *Alpine Symphony*, I always think back to how my time with Charlie made all of this possible for me. Thank you, Charlie!

Heinz Karl Schwebel
Professor of Trumpet, Federal University of Bahia;
Principal Trumpet, Bahia Symphony Orchestra

The year was 1988, I was eighteen years old, and it was the first time Charles Schlueter had come to Brazil to teach at the first Northeastern Brass Meeting. I remember seeing that man walking into the hall where the class was supposed to happen, smoking his pipe, wearing yellow pants and a blue polo shirt, and carrying a leather gig bag over his shoulder. Quite a view!

I was in for a two-week period of daily master classes with that man. The anticipation was overwhelming—after all, he was the principal trumpet of the Boston Symphony Orchestra.

The class began and, after talking extensively about breathing and sound for a whole hour, Charlie decided to demonstrate what he meant and started playing the *Trauermarsch* from Mahler's 5th—no warm-up necessary! Those first four notes were all it took to get me hooked on Charlie!

That sound was different than anything I had heard come out of a trumpet up to that point. Fuller, richer, more brilliant. Not that I could pinpoint all those characteristics at that early age. I could tell it was a different sound than all others I had heard before, but it would take me a few years to fully understand why it was different and why I liked it so much.

That first experience eventually led me to go study with Charlie at the New England Conservatory in Boston in 1994. I was a regular student of his for a total of four and a half years during my master's and doctoral degrees, and those years have shaped not only my trumpet playing, but also my general musical understanding as well as my love and respect for the profession.

I remember calling Charlie when I first arrived in Boston to schedule my lesson. I asked him what I should bring as far as music and methods go, and he told me to bring the Charlier and Walter Smith's *Top Tones* books. I felt pretty confident, since I had played many of those before, but I decided to be safe and practiced the first two studies in each book so I was sure I would do well on my first lesson. I should have known better! Charlie took the *Top Tones* and flipped it to "Etude No. 24 in D-sharp minor"! I couldn't play four notes without missing three of them! I was so embarrassed that I promised myself I would never let that happen again. But Charlie was very understanding and sympathetic with me that day, as he would be for the next four and a half years.

All students in Charlie's studio would normally get a one-hour lesson each week. Eventually, a two-hour lesson was necessary to compensate for a week Charlie couldn't teach for some reason. I made sure I had lots of questions for him on those long lessons! One hour or two hours long, lesson day was always the most anticipated day of the week! I was never late for my lesson; I could not wait to get in that room and play for him!

And play I did! He took me through many etude books besides the two already mentioned: Bousquet, Brandt, Harris, and Goldman, among many others. Etudes were a favorite tool of his. He thought they were a great vehicle for transmitting his concepts of sound, phrasing, articulation, how notes should be grouped and shaped, and music in general. He used to say to me, "The problem is, most people play etudes as if they were just etudes, not music." Another of his favorite sayings was, "Solve a technical problem musically." Etudes were great for approaching technical problems if you followed that advice.

Charlie would play a lot for us in our lessons to demonstrate his concepts. He did not bring his own trumpet; he used the student's horn and mouthpiece to do that. In my particular case, that didn't pose a problem for him because I used the same mouthpiece he did, but I know that was not the case with many others. It was pretty amazing to see him just pick up whatever horn and mouthpiece the student was using and sound like a million bucks! His explanation was very eye-opening for anyone with an interest in teaching. He said he wanted to make a point to the student that he (the student) could sound better no matter what equipment he was holding in his hands.

An aspect that was particularly admirable in Charlie's personality was his generosity toward his students. He would always find a way to sneak the interested ones into Boston's Symphony Hall to listen to BSO concerts for free. He must have saved me thousands of dollars in tickets, since I would show up at least twice for each week's program!

Lending his instruments was another way he helped lots of us! I recall using many of his horns and actually having one of his Monette C trumpets for my entire doctoral program! But lending wasn't enough! He would take time to build us horns! He built me an E-flat trumpet out of Getzen and Martin parts and a piccolo with the leftovers!

I remember when one of his former students entered my practice room one day at NEC, his face livid, showing me one of Charlie's C trumpets he had borrowed for a Tanglewood audition with its bell completely destroyed after he slipped on ice in front of the New England Conservatory and landed on top of his soft case!! He found the nerve to show it to Charlie, who simply said, "Oh well, take it to Ken Pope for now. I will send it to Dave later." Typical Charlie!

As much as studying and socializing with him was an incredible experience, nothing tops having listened to Charlie perform live with the BSO. That was the pinnacle of my trumpet education. Everything he would tell me to do in a lesson I could witness being practiced in real life!

I heard many world-famous orchestras when I was in Boston and many wonderful trumpeters. But listening to Charlie was always something special. That sound will never leave my mind!

I was lucky enough to hear him play all the big repertoire. All the Mahler symphonies, all the Strauss tone poems, *Pictures*, Prokofiev, Shostakovich, you name it! Charlie's posthorn solo on Mahler 3 was eye-watering!

My admiration for the man and the musician grew with each concert I heard! Listening to *Alpine Symphony* being performed at an evening concert, knowing he had rehearsed Mahler 2 the previous morning (that program was going to be presented at the upcoming BSO European tour, hence the morning rehearsal!), was jaw-dropping!

As a friend once rightly put it, "God broke the mold after Charlie." He's got one of the strongest personalities any trumpet player has shown, and he sure makes a point of letting you know that. Listening to him was a life-changing experience for me. I hope the new generation of students will find a way to enjoy—either through his now-seldom live performances, or through the scores of recordings out there—the brilliance of his playing I and so many others have had the privilege of experiencing! And if you youngsters find yourselves in the same room with him one day, go shake his hand and say hello. You will be, for a moment, in the presence of a legend!

Nailson Simões
Professor of Trumpet, University of Rio de Janeiro (retired)

In 1983, I met Professor Charles Schlueter in Dijon, France, during a brass festival. Although I had heard Mr. Schlueter's playing through his orchestral recordings, I was only able to meet him in person during that festival. I was fortunate enough to hear him soloing in Hummel's *Trumpet Concerto* with the festival's orchestra. His performance astounded me, as he approached the piece using new interpretative ideas I had never heard before. This encounter with Mr. Schlueter was a turning point in my life, not only for my musical career, but also as a human being.

My studies in the United States with Mr. Schlueter started in 1984 at Boston's New England Conservatory of Music, where I was pursuing a master's degree in trumpet performance. I was privileged to work under Prof. Schlueter's tutelage until 1991, when I completed my Doctorate of Musical Arts at the Catholic University of America in Washington, D.C. During those years, Mr. Schlueter traveled back and forth to Brazil, where he built a legacy throughout the entire country. Mr. Schlueter's legacy has left Brazil with an enormous influence, which had never happened before in the history of trumpet teaching in this country.

I am tremendously blessed and grateful for having such an innovative, courageous, extremely musical, and amazing person as my tutor. I owe my musical and personal life to Mr. Schlueter's influence. Every time I play with him, I learn something new, I feel humbled, and my admiration for him only grows with time. I would like to end by saying that my son, Nairam, who also fell in love with Mr. Schlueter's playing, holds a special admiration for him and, thanks to Mr. Schlueter, also considers him a mentor.

Matthew Sonneborn
Principal Trumpet, Naples Philharmonic

My name is Matt Sonneborn, and I have been the principal trumpet of the Naples Philharmonic since 1989. What a profound privilege it is to tell you a bit about my time with Charlie and the indelible mark he left on me and his studio. The bond between teacher and student is one that is difficult to describe, perhaps, to those that aren't in music as a career path. To this day, I hear Charlie's voice in every note I play, and I live my life from concepts that were developed cognitively in that room, with a music stand and two chairs in a small room, an hour at a time once a week.

The first thing that strikes you as different from other teachers you may have had is that Charlie quickly erases any barrier of judgement with you as a student. You aren't asked to prepare week-to-week new assignments but rather sight-read each lesson. He was clear that you were there to be helped, and that meant you had permission to make mistakes. What was highly emphasized was the freedom to be intensely engaged in the rules and concepts that he was imploring you to understand. This book will cover those in great detail.

His low voice would always be solfèging and singing along, the scent of coffee always coming from his thermos, and the scents of his pipes always present. We would embark on what would be a test of his patience, perhaps (though patient he was), as we went through the next series of traps I had not learned to avoid in a *Top Tone* or a Charlier. Eventually, it felt as if he was almost playing the trumpet for me, once I could truly immerse myself in the way of thinking he prescribed. It wasn't about playing the correct rhythms and pitches per se, but rather the correct groupings, thought process, and imagination that got me to do all that correctly. He emphasized less about embouchure and more about efficient air use.

If I was having a bad day and would check in with Charlie, he would usually say, "When is the last time you tried filling up your lungs to capacity and taking a goddamned breath?" and he was usually right that I hadn't, and that was usually all that was necessary.

I tried, after a while, to plan my lessons as the last of the day, which we dubbed "the pizza lesson" in my last year. Over those post-lesson sausage-and-mushroom pizzas, I was able to appreciate the profession a bit more and what it was for him to do the gig day in and day out. He was usually off to play a concert right after, and sometimes I would go to those incredible performances as well. Before one of those meals, his pipe lit outside, I said, "Charlie, when I am up there in that room in a lesson, I can play anything, but it's so hard to do on my own." He replied in his typical low mutter, "Maybe when I stop breastfeeding you, you'll figure it out ..."

When Charlie was on, there was nothing like it. The hair on the back of my neck would stand at attention, the hair on my face would pop out, and my mouth would pop open, and I would literally be mouthing "Holy shit!" and tears would flow down my cheeks! That, too, was the continuing of the lesson.

I tell all my students this story, too. In my first lesson, Charlie told me "The hardest thing about playing the trumpet is that it's so easy." Man, did that seem crazy. Now it makes so much sense. We try too hard. The analogies for life have spilled forth through that mantra. We overthink, we overanalyze. "Think in the present" is another Charlie mantra that serves me well in life. He made all music into a sort of hypnotic state of that clock that, instead of numbers, says now, now, now, now. He drew a picture on one of my Charlier etudes. It was a line with a bubble and then a continuing line. He described the bubble as a sort of hypnotic state representing when I was playing. There was an imaginary moving "highlighter" on the music, not too far ahead, but just enough to process the present in the entire piece. Suddenly, you knew you'd played, but in that time and space the music began and ended. This was the *Zen* that Charlie was able to teach and one of the great gifts he was able to impart. The whole while, that stentorian, wide, deep, basso singing, encouraging you to play with slow, hot air pervaded everything you'd played. You would hear him clear his throat, always a joke or two, and tell you something that embodied the survivor that he is.

Things were a bit of a battle for Charlie at Symphony Hall. That meant he also taught us the skills to cope with any extraneous distractions, like a conductor that wanted you fired. Charlie is a risk taker. He drives a bit like he plays. He tended to drive 90–100 mph to and from Tanglewood, always a rush to be his passenger. It reflected in his playing something impossibly loud or soft for the appropriate moments. The experience of being his student was nothing short of life-changing, and I thank him every time I pick up my horn.

Jim Stephenson
Composer; Second Trumpet, Naples Philharmonic (retired)

It's apropos that I'm writing about Charlie just after doing a recording session with him (at 78 years old and with a bruised rib!) of a new piece I composed for him and Marvin Stamm as soloists with the New England Conservatory Symphonic Winds. The piece is called "It's About Time."

The reason it's so timely is because the piece embodies so much about Charlie and what he has done for me personally.

I graduated from NEC with a degree in trumpet performance, but I write this paragraph now as a full-time composer. Yes, I played 17 years with a symphony orchestra, a professional accomplishment largely due, of course, to Charlie's teaching. But it was my post-trumpet career—composition—where Charlie has played a part more than anything. And this is because of his love and generosity for all of his students. When I think back to my college days at NEC, I remember a teacher who spent countless hours teaching tirelessly (I can still hear him yelling instructions while I played!), who would then go almost immediately to Symphony Hall for performance as principal trumpeter of the BSO. I remember someone who would only miss his students' recitals if he absolutely had no other choice due to concerts or other previous commitments (I know for a fact that he made all three of mine). In addition to a bit of coffee, pizza, and pipe aroma, the lessons were filled with anecdote after anecdote, all of which had meaning that went far beyond just their application to the trumpet. And the jokes too—always a new one right around the corner. One would think that when a trumpeter then decided to go another direction, such as into composition as I did, that the former teacher might lose interest. But Charlie has done quite the opposite. Through his foundation, he has personally helped to fund my early Trumpet Concerto #1 (which truly helped boost my career), another chamber piece for which he wished to remain anonymous, a duo trumpet work with band ("Duo Fantastique"), and then this latest one, "It's About Time." Not only did he support them, but he had to perform on two of them as well! And my music isn't easy! Generous and brave man!

Now that I am the age he was when I was his student, I'm especially impressed at how his well-documented BSO Ozawa "issues" never carried over into lessons. The time in the studio was always about the student, and what the student needed to improve as a player and human being. I'm truly honored, as I know everyone else is as well, to share publicly what a warm and caring man Charlie has always been. And so now that there is a book by Charlie, all I can say is, "It's about time!"

Andrew Stetson

Senior Associate Director and Associate Professor, Texas Tech University

Before I auditioned for the New England Conservatory, I made every possible attempt to get as much information as possible about Charlie, the man who would become my teacher. My goal was to sound exactly like what he would have wanted an auditioning student to be, and therefore impossible not to be accepted. I listened to recordings, met with current and former students, took lessons with some of them, and read interviews. During all this research, I came across some writing in which Charlie was asked, "What do you listen for when you are evaluating an audition?" I was perplexed at his answer, as it provided nothing concrete for me to put stock in as I prepared to audition for him. He answered, "I don't know, but I know it when I hear it." What was I supposed to do with that?

Luckily, Charlie did hear something he liked and accepted me into his studio. Soon I was to have my first lesson, still not knowing what he wanted or what to expect. I brought along a mountain of etude books, hoping I'd have the one he'd approve of. Months earlier, I had auditioned on Charlier No. 6, so I pulled that out, figuring it would be an excellent place to start. Charlie immediately flipped from No. 6 to No. 1.

"Have you done this one?" I had, and so he flipped to No. 2.

"How about this?" Again, I had, so he flipped to No. 3.

"This one?" I hadn't, and that's where my journey with Charlie began: sight-reading Charlier No. 3.

So we began. I played the first three notes and was emphatically implored to stop.

"No, no, no, short. The second note is short." I tried again.

"No, no, think of the end of that note." So, I tried that. I thought of the end of the note, having no clue what that entailed or what he was talking about, and began again.

This time, Charlie didn't say anything. Instead, he grabbed my trumpet and began playing the etude himself. It would be the first time I heard him play up close: my first experience with his sound. It was pure silk to me: smooth, connected, utterly indescribable.

"Like that," he muttered as if he had explained this all a thousand times before. "The end of the note contains everything you need, how the note is shaped, grouped, and connected." He went on in some detail, but my mind wandered away and back to his sound. I didn't know my trumpet could do that.

He handed my trumpet back to me, and it was my turn again. I set my inner dialogue to what would become my new mantra. "End of note. End of note. End of note," and I tried again.

"THAAAAAT'S IT!" he exclaimed as he added emphasis with a firm and painful pat on the back.

"It was?" I thought to myself, not wanting to argue with the praise I had just received. To me, I didn't do anything, just tried again.

With that, an hour had gone by, and the lesson was over—an hour to make it through the first line of the etude.

Thus began a four-year journey that would invariably include the same advice each and every lesson. Ending my notes, shaping everything, grouping it all together, connecting them with sound and silence. As his students, we would have heated discussions about what all this meant, whether it worked, why it worked, how we could make them work. We would have late nights at Cappy's Pizza (now closed), toiling and trying to figure it out. At some point, we were all frustrated by the same thing, namely, that we understood but couldn't consistently apply Charlie's concepts. We could never predict when we'd get that pat on the back.

In some ways, these were futile discussions. We were attempting to consciously explain concepts that weren't meant to work to our conscious minds at all. This was all much deeper, something that could match skill and talent with art and beauty in a part of our minds we had no access to. More than anything, the "Note End Concept" was meant to get us out of our own ways—to quiet our minds from all that they can obsess over and focus instead on something simple. It was one thing, one thought that could unlock all that music has to offer, but in the process, all that our unconscious minds' hearts can bring as well.

As a teacher and a scholar, I have now come up with many ideas about why all this works. I can describe how note endings can make the physical demands of the trumpet easier in the real world, and in some sense, much of this book will explain that to you as well.

But to this day, when I play in a way that would invoke that pat on the back, or an exclamation of "thaaaat's it" from the man whom I owe so much ...

I don't know how it happens, but I know it when it does.

Jeffrey Work
Principal Trumpet, Oregon Symphony and Colorado Music Festival Orchestra

My high school friend and mentor, John Findley, told me point-blank, "You've got to check out the Boston Symphony's new principal trumpet, Charlie Schlueter." In 1982, as my search for an educational home occupied me fully, the recommendation held weight. "Plenty of people can play the trumpet," my friend went on, "but this guy plays more musically than anyone I've heard!" Not long after, I remember sitting in Symphony Hall, hearing Charlie for the first time, wide-eyed and open-eared. The sounds that came out of his bell, so unbelievably vibrant and colorful, changed my view of trumpet playing—and music-making—for good. And *then* came the lessons!

The following year I became a "Schlueter student," and that phrase means a great many things to me to this day. For me, as a performer, it means I still tap my foot and shape the ends of notes and breathe like breathing is going out of style. It means I try to stay in the present, not focusing on recent mishaps or recent successes. It means I listen to the connections between the notes I play, including when those connections are silences. It means I play better, for some reason, whenever I smell pipe smoke and coffee.

As a musician, it means I try to forget all of that performer stuff and focus on touching people's hearts. It means I hear groups of notes like an actor hears the spoken word. It means I believe that technical problems have musical solutions. It means I have a sense of reverence for performance traditions and past greats of the instrument like my grand teacher William Vacchiano.

As a person, it means valuing my lifelong friendship with the man who started out as "Mr. Schlueter" and who became our beloved Charlie. It means enjoying his stories, whether they be old favorites or new additions. It means persevering through adversity. It means feeling grateful for the dedication and generosity he's always shown to his students.

Charlie Schlueter's artistic legacy has two parts, I think: the first, as a performer, rings in our ears as echoes of the indescribably beautiful things he achieved in the concert hall and on record. The second, as an educator, lives on and will grow in subsequent generations of trumpeters, giving us the widest palette of colors in our playing, giving us the tools to continually teach and improve ourselves, giving us the strength to soldier on through difficult times ... and the list goes on. Undoubtedly, as we're all given the chance to read his new book, Charlie will surprise us once again with some unforeseen insight, some new angle of approach, or perhaps some new view of our craft, our art, and our world.

Gene Young *(August 23, 1938 – June 19, 2018)*
Professor, Oberlin Conservatory; Director, Peabody Camerata at Peabody Conservatory of Music

Charlie Schlueter and I became friends when Charlie secured a position with the Cleveland Orchestra with George Szell as conductor. I was teaching at Oberlin College and its close proximity to Cleveland afforded many opportunities for Charlie and me to meet, speak, and discuss our many mutual interests (trumpet, orchestral playing, Vacchiano, musicianship, and a wide spectrum of ideas, concepts, and opinions). Most naturally, a friendship was formed.

Our friendship deepened as I witnessed Charlie's professional career develop, from Cleveland, to Minnesota, and on to Boston. An extraordinary succession of performances solidified Charlie's reputation as one of the greatest and most musical of all trumpeters, past and present.

Charlie's teaching, like his model William Vacchiano, is to be noted and admired. At Charlie's retirement ceremony, students traveled from as far as Brazil and Japan to acknowledge their teacher. A personal and direct approach to each student exemplifies Charlie's care in his teaching and his professional involvement with every individual. The trumpet world will be richer, as will the entire musical world, upon experiencing Charlie's writing. My friendship with Charlie has most certainly enriched my life and expanded my musical horizons.

Discography

Orchestral Recordings

Barber
- Violin Concerto, Boston Symphony with Seiji Ozawa and Itzhak Perlman

Bartók
- Concerto for Orchestra, Minnesota Orchestra with Stanisław Skrowaczewski
- Concerto for Orchestra, Boston Symphony with Seiji Ozawa
- Dance Suite, Minnesota Orchestra with Stanisław Skrowaczewski
- *The Miraculous Mandarin* (Suite), Minnesota Orchestra with Stanisław Skrowaczewski
- *The Miraculous Mandarin* (Complete), Boston Symphony with Seiji Ozawa
- *The Wooden Prince* (Suite from the Ballet), Minnesota Orchestra with Stanisław Skrowaczewski

Beethoven
- Overtures and Incidental Music, Minnesota Orchestra with Stanisław Skrowaczewski

- Symphony No. 5 and *Wellington's Victory/Egmont*, Boston Symphony Brass with New York Philharmonic and Canadian Brass
- Symphony No. 7 (Bernstein's Final Concert), Boston Symphony with Leonard Bernstein
- Piano Concertos, Boston Symphony and Rudolf Serkin

Berlioz

- Requiem, Boston Symphony with Seiji Ozawa

Brahms

- Symphonies Nos. 1, 2, and 3, Boston Symphony with Bernard Haitink
- *Variations on a Theme of Haydn*, Boston Symphony with Bernard Haitink

Britten

- Diversions, Boston Symphony with Seiji Ozawa and Leon Fleisher
- *Peter Grimes: Four Sea Interludes*, Boston Symphony with Carl St. Clair

Bruckner

- Symphony No. 8, Cleveland Orchestra with George Szell

Debussy

- *La Mer*, Boston Symphony with Colin Davis
- *Nocturnes*, Boston Symphony with Colin Davis

Dvořák

- *Carnival Overture*, Slavonic Dances, Boston Symphony with Seiji Ozawa

- Cello Concerto, Boston Symphony with Seiji Ozawa and Mstislav Rostropovich
- Symphony No. 8, Minnesota Orchestra with Neville Marriner

Gabrieli

- *Canzon in Double Echo*, Boston Symphony Brass with New York Philharmonic, Canadian Brass and Kazuyoshi Akiyama
- *Canzon Quarti Toni*, Boston Symphony Brass with New York Philharmonic, Canadian Brass and Kazuyoshi Akiyama
- *Canzon V, VI, X, XVI*, Boston Symphony Brass with Canadian Brass and Kazuyoshi Akiyama

Handel

- *Royal Fireworks Music*, Minnesota Orchestra with Stanisław Skrowaczewski
- *Water Music* (Suite), Minnesota Orchestra with Stanisław Skrowaczewski

Kirchner

- Concerto for Violin, Cello, Ten Winds & Percussion, Boston Symphony Chamber Players
- Music for 12, Boston Symphony Chamber Players

Liszt

- Piano Concertos, Boston Symphony with Seiji Ozawa
- *Totentanz*, Boston Symphony with Seiji Ozawa

Mahler

- Symphony No. 1, Boston Symphony with Seiji Ozawa

- Symphony No. 2, Boston Symphony with Seiji Ozawa
- Symphony No. 3, Boston Symphony with Seiji Ozawa
- Symphony No. 4, Boston Symphony with Seiji Ozawa
- Symphony No. 5, Boston Symphony with Seiji Ozawa
- Symphony No. 6, Boston Symphony with Seiji Ozawa
- Symphony No. 7, Boston Symphony with Seiji Ozawa
- Symphony No. 10 (Adagio), Boston Symphony with Seiji Ozawa

Mendelssohn

- *Midsummer Night's Dream*, Boston Symphony with Seiji Ozawa

Messiaen

- *Oiseaux Exotiques (Uchida)*, Boston Symphony with Seiji Ozawa

Monteverdi

- *Christmas Vespers*, Boston Symphony Brass with New York Philharmonic, Canadian Brass and Kazuyoshi Akiyama
- *Vespers of the Blessed Virgin*, Boston Symphony Brass with New York Philharmonic, Canadian Brass and Kazuyoshi Akiyama

Panufnik

- Symphony No. 8, Boston Symphony with Seiji Ozawa

Poulenc

- *Gloria*, Boston Symphony with Seiji Ozawa
- *Stabat Mater*, Boston Symphony with Seiji Ozawa

Previn

- Violin Concerto, Boston Symphony with André Previn and Anne-Sophie Mutter

Prokofiev

- *Peter and the Wolf*, Boston Symphony with Seiji Ozawa
- Piano Concerto # 4, Boston Symphony with Seiji Ozawa and Leon Fleisher
- *Romeo and Juliet* (complete), Boston Symphony with Seiji Ozawa
- *The Love for Three Oranges* (Suite), Minnesota Orchestra with Stanisław Skrowaczewski
- *Romeo and Juliet* (Suites 1 & 2), Minnesota Orchestra with Stanisław Skrowaczewski
- *Scythian Suite*, Minnesota Orchestra with Stanisław Skrowaczewski

Ravel

- *Alborada del gracioso*, Minnesota Orchestra with Stanisław Skrowaczewski
- *Alborada del gracioso*, Boston Symphony with Bernard Haitink
- *Une barque sur l'océan*, Minnesota Orchestra with Stanisław Skrowaczewski
- *Boléro*, Minnesota Orchestra with Stanisław Skrowaczewski
- *Boléro*, Boston Symphony with Bernard Haitink

- Concerto for the Left Hand/Fleisher, Boston Symphony with Seiji Ozawa
- *Daphnis et Chloé* (Complete), Boston Symphony with Bernard Haitink
- *Daphnis et Chloé* (Suites 1 & 2), Minnesota Orchestra with Stanisław Skrowaczewski
- *L'éventail de Jeanne*, Minnesota Orchestra with Stanisław Skrowaczewski
- *La Valse*, Minnesota Orchestra with Stanisław Skrowaczewski
- *La Valse*, Boston Symphony with Bernard Haitink
- *Menuet antique*, Minnesota Orchestra with Stanisław Skrowaczewski
- *Rapsodie Espagnole*, Minnesota Orchestra with Stanisław Skrowaczewski
- *Rapsodie Espagnole*, Boston Symphony with Bernard Haitink
- *Le Tombeau de Couperin*, Minnesota Orchestra with Stanisław Skrowaczewski
- *Le Tombeau de Couperin*, Boston Symphony with Bernard Haitink
- *Valses nobles et sentimentales*, Minnesota Orchestra with Stanisław Skrowaczewski
- *Valses nobles et sentimentales*, Boston Symphony with Bernard Haitink

Schubert

- Symphony No. 8 ("Unfinished"), Boston Symphony Orchestra with Sir Colin Davis
- Overture to *Rosamunde*, Boston Symphony Orchestra with Sir Colin Davis

- Symphony No. 9 in C Major, Cleveland Orchestra with George Szell

Sessions

- Concerto for Orchestra, Boston Symphony with Seiji Ozawa

Sibelius

- *Finlandia*, Boston Symphony with Vladimir Ashkenazy
- Symphony No. 2, Boston Symphony with Vladimir Ashkenazy

Strauss

- *Also Sprach Zarathustra*, Boston Symphony with Seiji Ozawa
- *Ein Heldenleben*, Boston Symphony with Seiji Ozawa
- *Don Quixote*, Boston Symphony with Seiji Ozawa and Yo-Yo Ma
- *Elektra*, Boston Symphony with Seiji Ozawa

Stravinsky

- *Firebird* (Complete), Boston Symphony with Seiji Ozawa
- *Firebird* (Suite), Minnesota Orchestra with Stanisław Skrowaczewski
- *Petrouchka*, Minnesota Orchestra with Stanisław Skrowaczewski
- *Le Sacre du Printemps*, Minnesota Orchestra with Stanisław Skrowaczewski

- *Le Sacre du Printemps*, Cleveland Orchestra with Pierre Boulez

Tchaikovsky
- *Nutcracker* (Complete), Boston Symphony with Seiji Ozawa
- *Nutcracker* (Suite), Minnesota Orchestra with Leonard Slatkin
- *Swan Lake* (Suite), Minnesota Orchestra with Leonard Slatkin
- Symphony No. 6, Boston Symphony with Seiji Ozawa

Wagner
- *Tannhäuser* (Overture, *Venusberg Music*), Minnesota Orchestra with Stanisław Skrowaczewski

Solo Recordings

Bravura Trumpet
- Ketting: *Intrada*
- Suderburg: Chamber Music VII—*Ceremonies*
- Chardon: Sonate pour trompette en ré et violoncelle
- Suderburg: Chamber Music VIII—*Sonata*
- Hindemith: Sonate

Virtuoso Trumpet
- Honegger: *Intrada*
- Enesco: *Légende*
- Chardon: Sonate pour trompette en ré et violoncelle
- Poulenc: Sonata for Horn, Trumpet and Trombone

- ☐ Saint-Saëns: Septet
- ☐ Svoboda: Duo Concerto

Trumpet Concertos
- ☐ Neruda: Concerto in E-flat
- ☐ Haydn: Concerto in E-flat
- ☐ Tartini: Concerto in D
- ☐ Hummel: Concerto in E

Trumpet Works
- ☐ Suderburg: Chamber Music VII—*Ceremonies*
- ☐ Hubeau: Sonata
- ☐ Suderburg: Chamber Music VIII—*Sonata*
- ☐ Hindemith: Sonate

Songs from the Heart
- ☐ Losey: *Zaraida Polka*
- ☐ Losey: *Addah Polka*
- ☐ Bellstedt: *Carnival of Venice*
- ☐ Goedicke: *Concert Etude*
- ☐ Anderson: *A Trumpeter's Lullaby*
- ☐ Gustat: *To the West Caprice*
- ☐ Clarke: *Sounds from the Hudson*
- ☐ Thomé: *Fantaisie*
- ☐ Erlanger: *Solo de Concert*
- ☐ Rimsky-Korsakov/James: *Flight of the Bumblebee*
- ☐ Goldman: *Scherzo*
- ☐ Bolter: *Marsha's Gift*
- ☐ Ewazen: *Symphonic Memories*
- ☐ Ewazen: *A Song from the Heart*

Statements

- Lomon: *Odyssey*
- Copland: *Quiet City*
- Persichetti: *The Hollow Men*
- Bolter: *On the Cusp*
- Hovhaness: *Prayer of Saint Gregory*
- Peaslee: *Nightsongs*
- Tiberio: *Statements*

Schlueter Students

Cleveland
- Jack Brndiar
- Robert Dolwick
- Jane Dunnick
- David Eaton
- Tony Lane
- Ada Pesch

Minneapolis
- David Chapman
- Lynn Deichert
- Lynn Erickson
- Larry Griffin
- Don Hakala
- Lester Monts
- Thomas Rolfs
- Byron Stripling
- Rob Walser

Boston — NEC
- Lillibeth Aycud
- Andrew Balio
- David Bamonte
- Stephen Banzaert
- Darren Barrett
- Rachel Bellairs
- Natalie Berg
- Eric M. Berlin
- Thomas Bithell
- Andrew Blais
- Eric Bloom
- Jaimie Branch
- Scott Bullock
- Melissa Bushee
- Charles Canney
- Nicholas Catino
- Michelle Claassen
- Sandra Clay

Joshua Cohen
Andrew Cormier
Scott Cowan
Thomas Cupples
Glaucio Da Fonseca
Antonio Dangerfield
Russell DeVuyst
Daniel Duncan
William Efflaudt
Mark Emery
Mireia Farres
Christian Ferrari
Colin Fisher
Mark Flegg
Thomas Fortier
Jason Gamer
Alysia Geiger
Michael Gettel
Angela Gosse
Michael Grandel
Nathaniel Hasterlik
Scott Hommel
Timothy Hudson
Eric Hyland
Jonathan Ingber

William Jaques
Nathan Joiner
Kenneth Jones
Cole Kamen-Green
Alan Kaschub
Peter Kenagy
David Killam
Sung-Hyun Kim
Dana King
Alessandra Kingsford
James Knabe
Dominique Koppe
Toshihiro Kosaka
Dean Laabs
Eric Latini
Erich Ledebuhr
Steven Lehn
Joseph Levinger
Janine Leyser
Sonja Lindsay
Andrew Littleford
Zachary Lyman
John MacDonald
Rodney Mack
Kerry MacKillop

Robert Massey
Brian McCreath
Andrew McGovern
Carl McGrier
Douglas McKenna
Nancy McPherson
Jimi Michel
Louis Milinazzo
Matthew Misener
Scott Moore
Robert Myers
Peter Myles
Sanh Nguyen
Dana Oakes
Vivek Patel
Paul Perfetti
Barry Perkins
Joseph Pero
Travis Peterson
Joseph Petrocelli
Karen Quast
Jonah Rabinowitz
Jennifer Rector
Casey Reeve
Ryan Resky

Waldron Ricks
Daniel Rosenthal
Darren Ruch
Roberto Ruiz
Jerry Sabatini
Christopher Schaetzly
Peter Schiller
Heinz Schwebel
David Secour
René Shapiro (Hernandez)
Carol Shier
Frederick Sienkiewicz
Robert Silverman
Andrew Simmons
Nailson Simoes
Matthew Small
Jeffrey Snyder
Matthew Sonneborn
Henrique Sousa Pereira
James Stephenson
Douglas Stephenson
Andrew Stetson
Christopher Still
George Stringer
Lauren Strobel

Phillip Sullivan
Mark Tannenholz
Geechi Taylor
Tsuyoshi Teramoto
Matthew Thomas
Joseph Tighe
Kevin Tracy
Eric Vismantas
Jeffrey Vom Saal
Komei Wakahara
Richard Watson
Ezra Weller
Diana Wensley
Michael Wentz
Pierson Wetzel
Seth Wish
James Wood
Jeffrey Work
David Workman
Byeong-Yeob Yu

Boston – Private

Madeleine Abromowitz
Daniel Bassin
Zach Botham
Mike Butler
Dennis Caron
Marsha Caron
Paulo Cilembrini
Justin Cohen
Mark Fenderson
Charlie Gasque
Paul Goldberg
Katsutoshi Kameshima
Richard Kelley
Wayne King
Jacob Klapholz
Joseph Kress
Koji Motomura
Floyd Oster
John Schnell

Just Intonation and *Equal Temperament*

Just intonation is tuning intervals and the notes of the scale in accordance with the naturally occurring ratios of the harmonic series. Intervals sound best when the frequencies of the pitches (Hertz value) are related by simple ratio. The simplest ratios are the first instance of that interval among the notes of the harmonic series. For example, the major 3rd is found between the 5th and 4th notes of the harmonic series, so its ratio is 5:4.

Variable-pitch instruments such as strings, brass, and voices intuitively tune using *just intonation* because that is where each interval sounds best to the ear: Tuning a chord or interval *justly* results in a "pure" or beat-less sound. This is because the pitch of each note matches the corresponding note in the harmonics of the other.

Equal temperament is a way to divide the octave into 12 mathematically equal half-steps, which came into general use between 1750 and 1800. In equal temperament, the *ratio* of the frequencies of each half-step is precisely $1:^{12}\sqrt{2}$ (or about 1:1.06). This method of tuning fixed-pitch instruments results in every musical interval being precisely the same in every key, although all of them are at least somewhat "out of tune" compared to *just intonation*.

Using the table below, compare *equal-tempered* intervals on the piano with *justly-tuned* intervals that occur in the harmonic series. The differences are given in *cents*, as found on a modern tuner. A *cent* is 1/100 of an equal temperament half-step.

Interval	Equal Temperament	Just Intonation	Difference	Ratio
Octave	1200	1200	0	2:1
M7	1100	1088	−12	15:8
m7	1000	969	−31	7:4
M6	900	884	−16	5:3
m6	800	814	+14	8:5
P5	700	702	+2	3:2
A4/d5	600	590	−10	45:32
P4	500	498	−2	4:3
M3	400	386	−14	5:4
m3	300	316	+16	6:5
M2	200	204	+4	9:8
m2	100	112	+12	16:15
Unison	0	0	0	1:1

Created by Fred Sienkiewicz, D.M.A.
Inspired by Larry Scripp, Ed.D, at the New England Conservatory of Music

Gustat Warm-ups

Recipes

Probably anyone (other than those of my students who suggested that I include some of my favorite recipes) reading a book about trumpet playing will wonder why this section is here. There are several reasons: Music is sometimes said to be food for the soul; likewise, food can be music for the body. Someone who is playing exceptionally well is sometimes said to be "cooking." Or, so-and-so is a really "tasty" player. A multicourse meal might be a "symphony of flavors."

There are many correlations between cooking and playing an instrument. Each can be fun. Each is a process (although cooking results in a product—until it is consumed). Each requires concentration, imagination, practice, and creativity.

For me it can also be relaxing. In fact, I first used cooking as a means of diversion: on days of a very difficult concert, instead of spending hours and hours practicing a particularly difficult part (and wearing myself out, driving myself nuts, and/or raising my anxiety level), I would try a new recipe. Usually, I would find one that would require a lot of concentration, a lot of preparation, or both. This would keep my conscious mind occupied, help me stay in the present, and, thereby, reduce my anxiety.

The end result, of course, was a very tasty, satisfying meal that the rest of my family and I could enjoy. I also received nourishment, which enabled me to be at my physical and mental best while also having enjoyed a process that produced satisfying results: dinner.

Now for a few of my favorite recipes ...

Soups

Curry Squash Soup (Gayle Bernstein)

Ingredients:

- 1 large onion, chopped
- 3 T olive oil
- 3 T curry powder (or more to taste)
- 1½ quarts chicken broth
- 3 medium apples, peeled, cored, and cut into small pieces
- 3 12-oz. packages frozen butternut squash

Directions:

- Sauté onion in olive oil with curry powder until soft and golden.
- Add chicken broth and apples.
- Cook until apples are soft.
- Add squash; cook until no longer frozen.
- Puree with handheld blender.

Greek Lentil Soup

Ingredients:

- 16 ounces (2 cups) brown or green lentils
- ½ cup olive oil
- 3 T minced garlic
- 1 large onion, minced
- 2 large carrots, chopped
- 3 stalks celery, chopped
- 2 quarts vegetable broth or stock
- 2 T dried oregano
- 1 t crushed dried rosemary
- 4 packets G Washington's® Rich Brown Seasoning
- 4 bay leaves
- 1 6-ounce can tomato paste
- Salt and ground black pepper to taste
- 1 T olive oil, or to taste
- 1 T balsamic vinegar, or to taste

Directions:

- Place lentils in a large saucepan, add enough water to cover by 1 inch. Bring to a boil and cook until tender, about 10 minutes, and either drain or save liquid to add to broth.
- Heat olive oil in saucepan over medium heat. Add garlic, onion, carrot and celery; cook and stir until the onion has softened and turned translucent, about 5 minutes. Pour in lentils, broth, oregano, rosemary, G Washington's Rich Brown Seasoning, and bay leaves. Bring to a boil. Reduce heat to medium-low, cover, and simmer for 10 minutes.
- Stir in tomato paste and season with salt and pepper. Cover and simmer until lentils have softened, 45 minutes to 1 hour, stirring occasionally.
- I add the olive oil and vinegar to each bowl when served.

Main Courses

Bourbon and Orange Beef

Ingredients:

- 1 pound beef round or flank steak, cut in shreds
- ¼ cup soy sauce
- 1 T rice wine
- 1 T bourbon
- 1 t sugar
- 1-inch piece ginger root, minced
- 6 T peanut oil
- 3 or more dried red chili peppers
- peel of one orange, cut in matchsticks
- 1 carrot, cut in matchsticks
- 2 celery stalks, cut in matchsticks
- 1 small can baby corn
- 1 can straw mushrooms
- 1 T sesame oil
- 2 T sesame seeds, toasted

Directions:

- Marinate beef in mixture of soy, wine, bourbon, sugar, and ginger for about 1 hour, turning frequently.
- Heat 3 T of peanut oil in wok, and stir-fry peppers and orange peel 30 seconds or until blackened.
- Add carrots, stir-fry 30 seconds, then add celery.
- Stir-fry about 1 minute and move to plate.
- Return skillet to heat and stir-fry beef in remaining peanut oil over high heat until well browned.
- Return vegetables to wok, add baby corn and straw mushrooms, and heat through.
- Blend in sesame oil.
- Transfer to serving dish and sprinkle sesame seeds on top.

Chicken in Hoisin Sauce

Ingredients:

- 2 whole chicken breasts—boned and cut into 1-inch cubes
- 6–8 scallions (green onions) cut into 1/2-inch cubes
- 1 T soy sauce
- 2 T sesame oil
- 1 T rice wine
- 6 cloves garlic, minced fine
- 1 inch fresh ginger, minced fine (or more if you like)
- 5 T peanut oil in wok
- 4 T hoisin sauce

Directions:

- Combine scallions, soy sauce, sesame oil, rice wine, and chicken. Marinate at least 15 minutes.
- Sauté garlic and ginger for 10 to 20 seconds.
- Add 4 T hoisin sauce; cook for around 1 minute.
- Add chicken and 1 T water.
- Stir-fry for at least 5 minutes.

Hot and Sweet Diced Chicken

Ingredients:

- 2 whole chicken breasts, boned and cut into ½-inch pieces
- 2 egg whites
- 2 t cornstarch
- 1 t salt
- 3 T peanut oil
- 5 dried red chili peppers
- 1 cup diced bamboo shoots
- 1 cup diced carrots, blanched 1 minute
- ½ cup diced water chestnuts

- 1 red or yellow pepper, cut into ½-inch pieces
- 2 T hoisin sauce or brown bean sauce
- 4 t sugar
- 2 T rice wine
- 2 inches fresh ginger root, minced
- 4 cloves garlic, minced

Directions:

- Combine chicken, egg white, cornstarch, and salt. Set aside.
- Heat peanut oil in wok, and stir-fry chili peppers until pungent and brown.
- Add chicken mixture, and stir-fry 30 seconds (or slightly longer).
- Add vegetables, and stir-fry another 30 seconds.
- Blend in remaining ingredients; cook, stirring, for 2 minutes.

Monkfish and Asparagus

Ingredients:

- 1½ pounds monkfish fillets, cut into 1-inch cubes
- 1¼ t sugar
- ½ t salt
- 3 large shiitake mushrooms thinly sliced (if dried, soak for 20 minutes in hot water)
- 1¼ pounds medium asparagus, trimmed and cut diagonally into ½-inch-long spears
- 3 T rice wine
- 1 t cornstarch mixed with 1 T cold water
- 2 T soy sauce
- 2 T peanut oil
- 2 T chili sauce, or a paste of minced garlic (4 cloves) and ginger (2-inch piece)
- 2 T hoisin sauce
- 1 large red pepper, thinly sliced

- 1 T catsup
- 3 scallions, thinly sliced
- 2 T sesame oil

Directions:

- In a non-aluminum bowl, toss monkfish with ½ t salt and ¼ t sugar.
- Blanch asparagus in salted boiling water for 30 seconds.
- Combine rice wine, soy sauce, chili, hoisin, catsup, 1 t sugar, and sesame oil.
- Stir cornstarch mixture into fish by hand, gently but thoroughly.
- Heat ½ t peanut oil in wok over high heat.
- Stir-fry fish in two batches (½ + ½, total = 1 t oil) — cook 4–5 minutes, or until opaque (remove all fish from wok).
- Add remaining 1 t peanut oil to the wok; stir-fry garlic and ginger 30 seconds; add asparagus, pepper, mushroom, and soy sauce mixture.
- Return fish to wok, toss in scallions, and stir until heated through.

Pesto

Ingredients:

- 2 cups lightly packed fresh basil leaves (remove stems)
- 1 cup extra virgin olive oil
- ¼ cup pine nuts
- 4 large cloves garlic, peeled and trimmed
- 1 t salt
- 1½ t crushed red pepper (dried)
- ½ cup freshly grated Parmesan cheese
- 2 T freshly grated Romano (pecorino) cheese
- Linguine, rotini, or your favorite pasta

Directions:

- Put the basil leaves, ½ cup olive oil, pine nuts, garlic, and salt in food processor bowl. Process until smooth (stop periodically and scrape down the sides of the bowl with a rubber spatula), about 20 to 30 seconds total. If garlic cloves are really big, cut in half so all chunks will be processed. (Alternatively, process the garlic first, then add basil, etc.)
- Place the other ½ cup olive oil in very small saucepan or butter melter with crushed red pepper. Heat slowly until pepper just starts to brown. Remove from heat and allow to cool.
- Transfer ingredients from food processor bowl to a large mixing bowl. Blend in the Parmesan and Romano cheeses with a large wooden spoon.
- Pour cooled olive oil through a small strainer (removing pepper flakes) into the bowl of pesto. Mix in thoroughly.
- After cooking pasta but before draining it, add a couple tablespoons of the hot, starchy water to the pesto. Stir in.
- Drain pasta. Spoon pesto over pasta. Sprinkle on more Parmesan cheese if desired.

This recipe makes enough pesto for about 6 servings of pasta and it takes under an hour from start to finish.

Risotto with Asparagus

Ingredients:

- 1½ cups arborio (or carnaroli) rice
- ½ cup extra virgin olive oil
- 1 medium onion, sliced
- ½ cup white wine
- 1 pound asparagus
- At least 6 cups chicken broth (or vegetable broth)

- ¾ cup parmesan, grated

Directions:

- Clean asparagus and discard hard ends.
- Cut the tender parts of asparagus stems into diagonal pieces about 1 inch long; keep the tips separate.
- Bring broth to a boil alone in a separate pot.
- Heat ¼ cup olive oil in large saucepan; add sliced onion and cook until transparent.
- Add asparagus pieces, stir, then add rice. Stir rapidly. When the rice is coated with oil, add the wine, allow to evaporate, then add broth 1 ladleful at a time (about ½ cup). The rice should never get too dry but also should not be drowned—just barely covered with liquid.
- After about ten minutes, add asparagus tips and continue to stir while adding broth.
- When rice is almost done (about 20–25 minutes), add the parmesan cheese and the rest of the oil. Add salt and pepper to taste. Mix well and serve very hot—eat immediately.

Seafood Pasta Salad

Ingredients:

- 1 pound mock crab (shredded)
- 1 pound tri-colored pasta (fusilli, rotini, gemelli, corkscrews, or whatever you prefer)
- 1 each red, orange, and yellow pepper, sliced as you like
- 1 medium Vidalia onion, shredded
- 1 medium daikon radish, shredded

Dressing:

- 1 14-oz. jar of mayonnaise or mayonnaise substitute
- 3 T extra virgin olive oil

- 3 T lemon juice
- 1 t dry mustard
- 2 t onion powder
- 2 t garlic powder
- 2 packs G Washington's Rich Brown Seasoning
- 3 T Old Bay® Seasoning
- 3 T curry powder
- 2 t celery seed
- ½ t salt
- freshly ground pepper

Directions:

- Combine mock crab, peppers, onion, and daikon. Let it sit for an hour or more.
- Cook pasta al dente, drain, then combine with mock crab mixture.
- Blend dressing ingredients, then add to pasta mixture.
- Add more seasonings to taste.

Ten Alarm Vegetarian Chili

Ingredients:

- ½ cup extra virgin olive oil
- 3 large onions, chopped
- 5 large cloves garlic, minced
- 1 28-oz. can tomatoes (ground peeled) and 3 cups water
- 1 each red, green, yellow, and orange pepper
- 10–12 jalapeños (or more and/or other hot peppers: habanero, cherry, cayenne, etc.), seeded and chopped. (Note: Wear disposable rubber gloves when working with these peppers!!)
- 1 pound tofu, extra firm or firm, drained, rinsed, and crumbled
- 1 t celery seed
- 1 T cumin seed, crushed or ground

- 1 4-oz. can chili powder (or more)
- 2 envelopes G Washington's Rich Brown Seasoning
- 1 t dried basil
- 1½ t salt
- ¼ cup Worcestershire sauce
- 1 or 2 portabella mushrooms, cut into 1-inch cubes
- 1 8-oz. package of seitan (optional)
- 1 15-oz. or 18-oz. can each of garbanzos, black beans, white kidney beans, dark red kidney beans, and light red kidney beans, drained
- 1 cup black olives, sliced
- 2 cups each of fresh broccoli flowerets, zucchini (cut into small cubes), green beans
- 1 small package frozen corn
- Red onion, chopped
- Monterey Jack cheese, grated
- Tabasco sauce

Directions:

- Heat olive oil in 8–10-quart heavy saucepan. Add onion and garlic, and sauté until golden brown.
- Add tomatoes, water, peppers, tofu, spices, salt, and Worcestershire sauce.
- Bring to a boil and reduce heat to lowest setting. Simmer uncovered (I use a spatter screen) for at least 8 hours, stirring frequently. (It is necessary to cook for this length of time to blend all the flavors, especially the peppers. This can be done the day before serving and allowed to cool overnight.)
- Reheat to a low boil, then add the canned beans and black olives. Add a little water if necessary.
- Reduce heat, and simmer at least 1 hour. Stir frequently.
- Add mushrooms, seitan, and the fresh vegetables, and simmer about 20–30 minutes. Stir frequently.

- Add frozen corn, and cook for another 10 minutes. Stir frequently.

Note: It is very important to stir frequently because by this time the chili is very thick.

Serve anytime. This recipe serves 6–8 people and takes 1–2 hours prep time, followed by 10+ hours cooking time. The chopped red onion and cheese can be added on top of each serving, and the Tabasco is for any masochists present.

White Clam Sauce

Ingredients:

- ½ cup extra virgin olive oil
- 4 large cloves garlic, minced
- 2 T flour
- 5 6.5-oz. cans minced clams, drained, reserving the clam juice (makes 2 cups clams, 2 cups juice); or use 1 pint of fresh, minced clams, tightly packed, and 2 8-oz. bottles of clam juice
- ½ cup white wine
- ¼ cup lemon or lime juice
- ¼ cup chopped parsley
- Salt and freshly ground black pepper, to taste
- 1½ t dried thyme

Directions:

- In a 2-quart saucepan, heat the olive oil, then add the garlic and cook over moderate heat for 1 minute. Whisk in the flour.
- Add the clam juice, white wine, and lemon or lime juice, stirring constantly.
- Add the parsley, salt, pepper, and thyme; simmer gently for ten minutes.

- Add the clams and heat through.

This recipe serves 4–6 people. It takes about 30 minutes to prepare the ingredients and just over 10 minutes to cook. It is delicious served over linguine.

Desserts

Madeleine's Mom's Banana Bread

Ingredients:

- 1 cup sugar
- ½ cup butter
- 1 t salt
- 2 beaten eggs
- 3 mashed bananas (the blacker and more disgusting, the better—this is the secret ingredient)
- 2 cups flour
- 1 t baking soda dissolved in 1 T water
- 1 package chocolate chips (I like milk chocolate best) or 1 package walnuts

Directions:

- Cream together butter, sugar, and salt.
- Mix beaten eggs and mashed bananas; add to sugar and butter and beat a little more.
- Add baking soda/water mixture. (Optional: add 1 t vanilla or 1 t almond extract)
- Stir in flour. (If adding chips or nuts, first stir in 1 cup flour, then add chips/nuts, then add second cup of flour)
- Pour batter into well-greased bread pan (or three well-greased mini bread pans). I use muffin pans with liners.
- Bake at 350°F for 1¼ to 1½ hours. For muffins, bake about 30–35 minutes.

- Bread may be very brown and moist when done, but the top should look dry, and a toothpick should come out clean (except, maybe, for chocolate!)

Pecan Pie

Ingredients:

- 3 large eggs
- ½ c dark brown sugar
- ½ t cinnamon, ground
- ¼ t allspice, ground
- ½ t nutmeg, ground
- ⅛ t cloves, ground
- 1 c dark corn syrup
- 3 T butter or margarine, melted
- ¼ t salt
- 1½ t vanilla extract
- 2 c whole or chopped pecans
- 1½ T all-purpose flour
- 10-inch unbaked pie shell

Directions:

- Combine the first 10 ingredients and mix well.
- Blend pecans with flour and stir into the mixture.
- Turn into a 10-inch unbaked pie shell.
- Bake in preheated hot oven (400°F) for 15 minutes.
- Reduce heat to moderate (350°F), and bake 40 minutes longer or until a knife inserted in the center comes out clean.

Pumpkin Pie

Ingredients:

- 1 cup (dark) brown sugar
- 1 T flour
- ½ t salt

- 1 t ginger, ground
- 1 t cinnamon, ground
- 1 t fennel, ground
- ½ t nutmeg, ground
- ⅛ t black pepper, ground (optional)
- ¼ t cloves, ground
- ½ t allspice, ground
- ½ t mace, ground
- 3 large eggs
- 1½ cups pumpkin puree (1 can, unspiced)
- 1 cup light cream or undiluted evaporated milk
- 10-inch, unbaked pie shell

Directions:

- Mix together the first 11 ingredients.
- Beat in eggs.
- Stir in pumpkin and milk.
- Pour into unbaked pie shell.
- Bake in preheated hot oven (400°F) 50 to 60 minutes or until a knife inserted in the center comes out clean.

Acknowledgements

The most immediate acknowledgements must be for my students who have had a direct hand in helping me finish this book: Jimi Michel for being my indefatigable editor; Natalie Lewis for being my helpful assistant editor; Andrew Stetson for great graphics and formatting; Eric Berlin for many very important editorial suggestions; Matthew Sonneborn and Daniel Rosenthal for superbly illustrating the use of the concepts on familiar etudes; and last but certainly not least Justin Cohen, whom I have known longer than it took to write this book and to whom I will be forever grateful for his expertise as a proofreader extraordinaire. And then thank you to all the rest of my students from the last half-century, listed at the end of the book, from whom I learned so much about creating an environment that allowed them to teach themselves.

I am also grateful to Julie HawkOwl for her copyediting, Bill Holden and Ejyo Katagiri for their graphics assistance, and Faith Seddon for design development and input. My apologies to anyone whose name may have been inadvertently omitted.

Alas, most of those who have had a huge influence on me and from whom I learned about music, the trumpet, and life in general, have already passed on. That list includes all of my teachers—Charlie Archibald, Don Lemasters, Ed Brauer, Mel Siener, Bill Vacchiano, and Eloise Ristad—as well as many friends and colleagues, including especially Gene Young and Tom Stevens.

Another person who had a substantial influence on my life and learning is Dan Myers. He made me aware of the work of Milton Erickson and Murray Bowen, and he provided the catalyst for integrating self-hypnosis, using the unconscious mind, differentiating in relationships and cumulative learning, and handling anxiety, all within the proverbial wisdom that the whole is greater than the sum of the parts.

I must acknowledge the genius of David Monette, whose renovations in trumpet and mouthpiece design allowed, encouraged and enabled me to pursue what I achieved in tone and expression in music-making over the last two decades of my professional career.

And finally, I would be remiss if I didn't acknowledge Carl Vigeland for publishing *Indirection*, which he predicted (indirectly) over 30 years ago in his book, *In Concert*, that I would write.

www.ingramcontent.com/pod-product-compliance
Lightning Source LLC
Chambersburg PA
CBHW071738150426
43191CB00010B/1619